Contents

Management in The Police Service -First Line Management for Police Officers

by

D. Wainwright
and
N.A. Smith

Barry Rose
Chichester and London
1978

Published by
Barry Rose (Publishers) Limited
Little London, Chichester, West Sussex.
Printed in England by
T.J. Hunt Limited
62 Hatcham Road, Peckham, London SE15 1TW

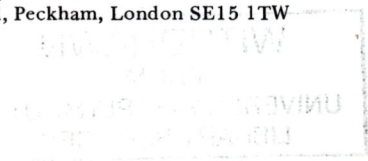

The Practical Man's Approach

This book is about management: the term "man management" does not appear, for whilst manpower is indisputably the most important of police resources, it is not the only one. The particular organisational structure and the ways in which resources such as buildings and vehicles are managed affect manpower; the attitudes of people and their job performance affect the ways other resources are used and the organisation functions.

If the theorists are to be believed, the techniques of managing people are so numerous and complicated that the practical manager may be forgiven for reaching the conclusion that by the time he has studied the divine science, he will have no time left for actually managing. Even if he can sort out the many conflicting theories and understand all the jargon, he may still feel they are addressed to people far above his head; those with the authority to implement them, and to get his boss to implement them as well. Life for the practical manager on the shop floor is not theoretical at all, they are real people he deals with, and he meets them face to face amidst the clatter of his daily work. At the same time, to be effective, no one can manage by the seat of his pants too long, there must be some plan to tackle the problems of people in an organisation. This book sets out a plan, without any claim that it is foolproof, or that it deals with every eventuality — such a system can be developed only in the light of each manager's knowledge, experience and commonsense.

Cynics say that management is "getting others to do what you can't do yourself", and, as with many cynical comments, it has a grain of truth. The manager's task is to organise all the resources at his disposal, which may well include skills and knowledge he does not possess himself. It is a lucky policeman who is a better photographer, dog handler, vehicle examiner, and detective then anyone else. No manager need feel ashamed that other people have better skills: his greatest contribution is a high degree of skill in managing people within the framework of his organisation, and this is the key — it acknowledges the individuality of each member of that organisation. It also creates the major problem, how to treat people as individuals within a formal organizational structure. Subordinates know the answer — they know they have to conform in important areas, otherwise the police service would not function, and few policemen are anarchists at heart. What irritates are situations which put unreasonable demands upon them, or ignore their rights as individuals. No one forgives attacks upon their dignity and self respect.

It's not suggested that Standing Orders be thrown through the nearest window, but are they issued for the smooth running of the organisation or as a threat of what will happen if people do not conform? Why are there laws? Not just to keep policemen in employment. Managers whose only strength is the book of rules are a menace — their way is stagnation and inefficiency: people want to be led, not bludgeoned, drugged or blackmailed. Every effective manager knows it, and whilst he recognizes that sometimes people need a push, he has a range of techniques to produce what is expected of him. They are listed below; the chapters fill in the detail.

1. The Organisation

Whatever reasons people may have for being in any organisation, they are there to carry out its functions and achieve its objectives. This is fairly easy where the personal aims of people and those of the organisation coincide. Structures of organisations create problems for those within them, particularly when they have grown without planning or are overdue for a major overhaul; in rare cases, the very structure itself and the methods it enforces may make the achievement of its objectives impossible, though the blame will fall on the managers for not trying hard enough. Practical managers are stuck with the organisation they have got — changing it is difficult, but every manager should know something of what it is, particularly where stress and friction are likely. He should know how his particular responsibilities fit into the pattern, what his objectives are, and where to direct his resouces for the best results. Managing people in an organisation is not just keeping them happy — it is keeping them happy and working for the organisation.

2. Motivation

People have needs such as status, esteem and satisfaction, and they look to their jobs to provide them. If it does not, they will channel their energies into something which does, so the practical manager does his best to ensure that their needs are satisfied in the work they do. It is easier to control a bunch of self starters — if they can be kept in check — than a group who have to be told what, when, where and how to do things, those who lack drive, initiative and all the other desirable qualities. Motivation is about turning people on, for no matter how smart the manager, people can't be supervised all the time. Promotion and job satisfaction are long term motivators, but encouragement and a pat on the back are equally important. Those who believe the old way is best: no pandering, grown men should not need praise, etc., should remember that any manager is only as good as the pile he sits on top of and that his success depends upon their performance. And a word of praise costs nothing.

3. Leadership
Modern theory rightly places emphasis on fair open leadership, but an effective leader can be ruthless and display low cunning, he can recognize the times when he must be harsh for the good of the job, and he does not hesitate to play these roles. He knows that he is going to be faced with problems that won't respond to unrelieved sweetness and light, but he keeps such situations to a minimum because he knows it closes the door on communication with his group, although he'll never use that as an excuse for neglecting what cries out to be done. The test of leadership is the ability to achieve the objectives given to him by the organisation, and once he senses how his group thinks and reacts to situations, he can lead successfully even though the group doesn't particularly like him.

4. Discipline and Morale
These are so related, it pays to consider them together. Much has been written about morale in organisations, complicated forms have been designed to reveal it, tables produced to quantify it, yet it remains as elusive as ever. Less complicated is the question "do they do the job willingly and well, and if not, what stops them?" No manager will find all the answers, but if he is leading his group well and the communication lines are wide open, he'll find out far more than the graduate psychologist. Discipline is essential to morale; no one really likes working for a slack outfit despite what they say, nor do many wish to labour under the constant threatening shadow of the rule book. Discipline is not punishment, which is a failure of discipline: the old adage that "rules are for the guidance of the wise and the obedience of fools" has a lot of

truth. But there are times when firm decisive action is needed, the practical manager has the courage to take it, because provided he is just and fair, he will be understood, supported and forgiven. And in matters of the fashionable self discipline, the manager must set an example.

5. Communication
So much lip service has been paid to communication it is in grave danger of becoming a stale joke. That would be a pity: the ability to communicate ideas, enthusiasm and instructions is an essential skill for every practical manager. The ability to communicate confidence, its use to motivate and develop team spirit is often overlooked. Communication is two way traffic, it is understanding and listening more than writing and speaking, in short, it is an awful lot more then telling people what to do.

6. Decision Making
All practical managers make decisions, the rules and instructions don't always say what the correct answer should be. The organisation puts constraints on possible decisions, all managers say "wouldn't it be nice if only . . . ". These constraints, such as the boss's bloodymindedness, are just factors in the process, not excuses why decisions shouldn't be made. Decision making is nothing more than accurately identifying the problem, weighing up all the factors and sorting them out. It can be a heavy responsibility, the practical manager knows he won't be right all the time though that doesn't stop him trying. But he can be reasonable.

7. Delegation
Delegation gives responsibility to subordinates, it satisfies their need to feel part of the activity in which they are involved. Practical managers know they cannot do everything themselves, they know those who try are as big a nuisance as those who sit back and do nothing: overworked, flustered people soon lose their sense of priorities. There are risks — subordinates are not always going to be successful, but if they are to be trained, gain experience, it is a risk practical managers know they must take — they know someone took it with them or they would not be where they are. They try to reduce the risk by delegating properly, and if looking round, they think there is no one capable enough to delegate to, they know they have failed in their other responsibilities such as training.

8. Assessment & Appraisal

Assessment is a constant activity which reveals subordinates to practical managers. If assessment is not continuous, there's an assumption that subordinates' performances never vary, that people are static and lifeless. Any manager who is that disinterested will get a variation — for the worse. Assessment is not just looking for improvement, it is creating it. Waiting for the annual appraisal, the snap five minutes on 'what we've been doing' is for historians, not practical managers. Appraisal interviews give people their chance to talk about their hopes and fears, what they want from the job and how they expect to get it. They can discuss what their overall performance has been, set the record straight if they think it is wrong. They expect criticism if below standard, as long as it is productive. Appraisal is not the grand slam annual rebuke — nobody's one hundred per cent useless.

9. Training

Courses and training departments may be excellent, though practical managers know the main responsibility for training rests on them. The nature of the policeman's job dictates it has to be learnt through doing it — for example, no classroom can create the horror and chaos of a motorway pile up. Training is improving job performance, increasing theoretical knowledge and practical ability, widening experience — it is putting people in situations from which they can learn, then making sure that they have done so. Training is positive, it is the manager's responsibility to train, not people's to blunder around hoping to pick the job up.

10. Development of the Individual

No industrial manager worth his salt leaves machinery and materials under-used, and the same should apply to people. Everybody has strengths and weaknesses, the practical manager's job is to make the best of them so that people feel whatever it is they are offering is being used. Most jobs have a fair share of routine, people accept it more readily if they know that an occasional piece of the real action will come their way, and they will be trusted to get on with the job.

10

1 *Organisation*

The Old Firm

When human beings come together to reach a common objective, they set up some method of doing it. Should that objective be continuing or long-term, a permanent method takes shape in which responsibilities are allocated, tasks defined, and information channels established. The organisation they create may be a social club, a government, a manufacturing company, a gang of criminals or a police force. How they shape the organisation will depend on many things, though generally the design will be so that the objectives can be best achieved.

As society expands, its objectives grow, becoming more complex. This is reflected in the organisations through which society reaches for its objectives: governments create new departments or change established ones, industries manufacture new products by advanced technologies, police forces adopt new techniques for traditional and additional roles, even gangs of criminals have to change. The control and coordination of organisations as they change direction or grow larger creates problems for everyone within them.

All practical managers consider their own organisation from time to time, what its objectives are, the way it functions, and whether the structure supports the relationship between the two. All managers are aware, sometimes painfully, of the strengths and weaknesses of their organisation, there are few who do not think occasionally that the carpets are greener on the other side of the street. Like many things in management, the workings of organisations are open to argument and discussion. Managers should be aware that some of it stems from the position adopted when looking at the picture.

It would help managers if there was one set of rules which applied to all organisations, national, local, public, private, service or manufacturing. Unfortunately, what works for one quite happily would be sudden death for another; a police force would not work on the same structure as a social club, even though some of the customers would not object. Yet both are human systems, created by, run by and operated for the benefit of people. Obviously, it is prudent to design the structure of any organisation according to the load it will have to bear and the constraints placed upon it.

If there are no rules, there are common factors which are the basis of most organisational structures, though it will always be open to argument which is best in any set of circumstances. Understanding these factors points to something about the management of organisations.

There are also external constraints upon organisations which effect the structure. All organisations exist as part of society and cannot be immune from it. Increasingly, legislation lays obligations on commercial enterprises and new responsibilities on public ones. The structure must be able to cope. As well as statutory restraints, there are others which may be more powerful; a company making wigwams by a method which produces clouds of evil-smelling smoke will not escape for long before there is some public reaction to its activities. Adjustment may be necessary within the existing structure by better control or new equipment. Or, new staff may be appointed, a new department created to deal with health and safety or environmental effects, it may re-site the factory at a location chosen in response to public opinion on the environment and employment prospects. Any police force is sensitive to public opinion, more so perhaps than other organisations. This affects the structure. Community relations officers and public relations officers are appointed to specialise in what are comparatively new fields. The expansion of any organisation creates extra pieces for the structure. How and where they are tacked on will determine the ease with which they function, whether they are grouped naturally or whether so many have been tacked on one side the whole structure begins to crack or lean under the strain.

All organisations need to reappraise their structures at some time. Many, like Topsy, just growed, and as a result may have developed in the wrong direction or lost touch with their original objectives. Amalgamations and take-overs present opportunities for reappraisal or force them on organisations, though it is not an exercise to be recommended too often, otherwise the organisation is in such a state of flux that managers become more occupied with keeping abreast of the changes than getting on with their prime task, that of running the show.

Because of the complexities of the original objectives, a decision is made in the early design stages of an organisation to separate various activities into easily defined groups. The more usual ways of making these divisions are:

By product or service. – In a manufacturing industry all those responsible for one product will be grouped. Those making cabbage strainers will be a separate group from those making rhubarb trimmers, even though they use the same skills, the same materials and work in the same buildings. Internal groupings are not always apparent to the casual observer. Each group will have personnel for purchasing raw materials, and the production and sales of the finished product. In the same organisation there will duplication of functions within the groups. The same grouping system can apply to services, typing pools and office services, for instance, may be centrally placed to serve the whole organisation. There are no set rules, one of the main problems in some industries is the decision to centralise or diversify. If expensive equipment is necessary, and even common typewriters are not cheap by the dozen, diversification may lead to inefficient use of equipment, particularly where a group cannot utilise it full time. Diversification of office services and typing would depend on its location in relation to the other groups to make it effective. The argument becomes more cogent when more expensive equipment such as computers or specialised transport is considered. Cost may force the decision to centralise on management, whatever structure it would like to have. Whatever decision is taken, there are other effects besides duplication and location. Managers like to have more common services, such as typing, under their own control. Groups have their own way of writing letters, their own reports, which it may be difficult to implement when control lies outside it. Large service groups may be inclined to impose restrictions, while operating within the structure for their own ends. Police managers are not the only ones who complain that form filling and admin is regarded by some as more important than getting on with the job of keeping the peace; industrial managers complain that the failure to send in returns promptly seems to cause greater concern than hold ups in the raw materials for rhubarb trimmers. There is always a danger when service departments, particularly, create objectives of their own and bend the structure towards their attainment.

By function. – This is perhaps the most widely used system of grouping. In industry the main functions of production, finance, personnel and sales are grouped together and will operate whatever the product being made; the same people being concerned with both cabbage and rhubarb trimmers. Grouping by function brings together all the knowledge and specialisation to make that function more effective. Police forces are grouped by function for operational purposes into C.I.D., Traffic and Uniform patrol. The relevant importance of each functional group within any organisation will vary with the nature of the work the organisation is engaged in; for instance, stock control will play a greater part in a mail order company than in an estate management company. This type of grouping avoids duplication of skills and equipment, it encourages standardisation within particular activities, and it strengthens any organisation where particular skills or knowledge are vital, not only because of the methods it will use, but also because of the accumulated information and experience the group will possess. By concentrating on one type of problem, the group should be come more adept at solving them. This is the basis on which criminal investigation and traffic departments are created, with what may generally be accepted as a fair degree of success. The disadvantage of this type of grouping is the difficulty people may find in relating their work to that of other groups and the objectives of the organisation as a whole. A traffic man will see the relationship to policing in general, although his horizon may be limited to his own department, confined in fact by the very specialisation which makes him an asset to the organisation. This will lead to a tendency to identify mainly with his group, in extreme cases at the expense of a sense of belonging to the organisation. A similar problem may arise within other groups when faced with functions out-side their specialisation; in cases where action is necessary they may fail to take it because of lack of knowledge or identification. This may be embarrassing in some organisations, it is non-productive when taken to the point where traffic men fail to take action on crime because it is the function of another group.

The coordination of functional grouping is more difficult than other types, partly because of the strengths of the groups. They themselves may be the only people with knowledge accurate enough to say what is possible and what is not. Possible in this context can mean desirable for the group. Remoteness of control, through distance or effectiveness, does hinder cooperation in some organisations.

By Territory. — Where the services provided extends over an area, groups are formed to provide the service in different parts of that area, the territorial divisions of a police force are prime example. This style of grouping fits most naturally into service or marketing structures, its most common problem being accurately to locate the group for greatest effectiveness, which leads to the definition of the group areas. Depending on the type of service, the groups will be located usually in large concentrations of customers or demand. It is possible to service supermarkets with wholesale supplies of cabbage strainers and rhubarb trimmers from one location. In times (if you'll forgive the simile) when they're selling like hot cakes, it will be expedient to have regional depots for better supplies. Where organisations are competitive, overlapping is to be expected. Where the service is non-competitive, boundaries between the groups are sometimes created artificially, in the case of police forces, usually by accepting local government areas. This may have disadvantages to the effectiveness of the grouping if the definition of area does not coincide with effectiveness of function; for instance local government boundaries are rarely drawn up with efficient policing in mind, yet they often define the areas of groups of policemen. Grouping by area can lead to duplication of resources, the spreading of expertise and equipment too thinly to be effective. There are also inherent problems of control and coordination, distance may make hearts grow fonder, though only as long as they can be trusted not to play to their own rules.

By Time. – Organisations which have objectives requiring round-the-clock attention group by time, the shift system. This allows the use of resources to meet the same or different levels of demand throughout the day and night. This is usual in every police force. Rigid grouping by time can lead to inflexibility, where for instance the groupings are identical irrespective of demand throughout the twentyfour hours. In fact, in most organisations there are differences in the type of work done by day and night, every policeman knows it. Where part of the organisation does not work throught the twenty-four hours, the inter-action between the groups will condition the type of work. It is, for instance, unusual for finance and personnel functions to be carried on round the clock. In one organisation long computer runs are done in the evening because of the absence of queries from other groups. Time groupings may conceal different functions, although the jobs may have the same names, and time groupings may be permanent, many people work permanent nights.

By line and staff. – Strictly speaking, this is grouping by function, but the expressions may have particular relevance in a police force, for the army were leaders in this method of classification. As warfare became more complex, supplies for the fighting troops became as important as putting them on the field of battle. Napoleon had it right when he declared that an army marched on its stomach, so the organisational structure of a brigade branched into two distinct types of management: line officers who controlled the activities of the fighting troops, and staff officers who ensured the fighting troops were supplied with bullets and bully beef. This division between line and staff is now common in most organisations. In the police service many staff functions are performed by non-police personnel, allowing the operational officers, the line units, to concentrate on the objectives of the organisation. In certain branches of the armed services staff far outnumber line personnel; some people believe the same situation will soon be reached in the police. In practice the division is not always so clear cut. Is crime prevention line or staff? It may be argued that it does not matter about classification if the job gets done. The distinction may be important in placing crime prevention in its correct place in the structure to ensure it is in the right area of command and responsibility. The place may be important for those doing the working when entitlement to allowances is considered. In many organisations, line people feel entitled to the lion's share of what is going, rather looking down on staff wallahs in their comfy offices. Staff groups are not entirely unresponsible, they are prone to set objectives such as good administration which they hold more dear than those the line officers should be helped to achieve. In many ways it is sad, neither can exist without the other, and the traditional antipathy where both groups seek their own importance at the expense of the other does-not eradicate these tendencies in which the real organisational objectives become hazy.

It would assist managers to understand groupings if organisations restricted themselves to one type. Unfortunately, many including a police force, will group by service, function, time and territory across line and staff demarcations when building up the structure. The usual way to understand the structure of any organisation is to create a model so those inside and out can recognise it and predict the way it might be expected to operate. The models, often referred to as family trees because of the pattern of branching used to illustrate divisions of a family through marriage, suggests answers to many questions on the organisation's structure; it places people in relation to one another by rank, role, and responsibility, it sets out their span of control. Fig. I shows part of the structure model of a police force.

The grouping may appear to raise problems. For instance, the territorial commander is responsible to all three Assistant Chief Constables for his functions, though not everything fits neatly into threefold classification; the arrest of a drunk and incapable which went wrong for instance, it's not crime, certainly not traffic and hardly administration. This is not flaw-finding, the organisation works and the model purports to show how; it suggests the absence of problems.

Fig. II shows the same officers with the groupings, and thereby responsibilities, changed. The problems of the territorial commanders may have been solved, those of the functional departmental heads may have been increased, they will now have to deal with three separate ACC's to have the same policy implemented throughout the force.

Fig. III is an extension to divisional level of Fig. I. Is the divisional traffic inspector responsible to his territorial commander only, or has he responsibility for some functions, line or staff, to the departmental commander? If so, the lines on the model do not indicate the possibility of strained loyalty through differing objectives and incompatible instructions. The divisional detective chief inspector faces similar problems. Is it correct to draw the conclusion from that model that the C.I.D. is more important because of the rank of its leader, or the responsibilities are greater although he commands less men? Is it correct to draw the conclusion that the responsibilities of a territorial commander are equal to those of a departmental commander, even though the latter directly controls a fraction of the number of men?

The model shows the span of control, or the number of people directly controlled by each manager. The more routine and repetitive the task, the greater the number of people who can be effectively controlled; the less the experience and knowledge of those people, the fewer the number in an effective span. If detailed control is necessary, the nature of the task will impose limits on the span of control. Close control may be restrictive, research and development departments need creativity, unusual answers to usual problems; certain aspects of police work have to be right, first time, every time. Each organisation had to consider its space and decide how they will help towards the objectives. Sometimes the confusion between spans of control and responsibility prevent either being right. Responsibility is for a function and the people who carry it out; span of control is responsibility for immediate subordinates.

Any organisation which is going to function successfully on a large scale must have a structure co-ordinating the activities of the different departments. Usually, this is achieved through the division of responsibility on the hierarchic basis of authority linked with power — the hire perspire and fire system — one level answering to another with each, hopefully, having clearly defined responsibility and activities. The ultimate form of this structure is the traditional bureaucracy on Civil Service lines based on close monitoring of each individual's activities. This form of structure has its drawbacks, loss of flexibility, penalisation of thoughtful unorthodoxy, tortuous adjustment to change and remoteness between decision makers and decision implementers. However, they do produce role stability and continuity which ensures the survival of the organisation regardless of the changing population within it. Many people, whilst complaining loudly and often about bureacratic structures are willing to pay the prices of loss of freedom for the comfort of working within them, they require less originality, less thought and less effort for managers, just a thorough knowledge of the rules and procedures.

In recent years many experiments have been carried out in controlling organisations through allowing greater participation in the effective decision making process. One company is run by a commonwealth and committee of workers/owners, another factory system is based on automatic working groups and a third is based on joint consultation. Even in these seemingly ideal organisations, there are of course many rules and regulations to be obeyed and research indicates that some members of them believe they are as fully bureaucratic as hierarchic organisations. Whilst there are marked differences of opinion among those promoting new systems about the ideal structure, some common ground exists, that people working within the organisation want to be involved, want a say in what affects them, including the organisational structure, they expect management to consider how people feel, think and act; and they also agree that these wishes aren't satisfied by putting a couple of workers on the Board of Directors, or granting better access to the Works Manager for the shop stewards.

The lines which link the parts of the model are also lines of communication. A person who has never seen such a model may be forgiven for thinking that communication is only vertical, people of equal rank never communicate, nor does group with group except by a very circuitous route. He may also wonder about the problems of coordinating and control when all those lines meet at the top.

Placing people in little boxes indicates their role in the organisation, what in fact they do. Role is not the same as authority, important roles, particularly in staff groups, may lack the authority of line managers. Where there is disparity of authority with equality of responsibility, the strong may dominate the weak, empires are built, the weak, line and staff are absorbed into them. Authority may be personal, or based on some traditional system such as seniority. Either way, our novice may be yet again forgiven if he thinks that all roles on the same level are equal.

The family tree may show the division between junior, senior and middle management. All enterprises exist in a changing society, common sense dictates that it is better to forecast change and make preparations rather than be faced with it when it arrives, having to accept whatever is expedient. Such action is only for chameleons. The best equipped to gaze into the future are senior management, they have the information at their disposal, they set the policy. Forward planning depends on the nature of the organisation, it can be a year ahead, or in the case of the Forestry Commission, fifty years. Middle management's planning horizons are set by those of senior management, they should be well versed in the policy and structure of the organisation, as minor policy changes are often left to them. Day to day problems are dealt with by junior management, which is closest to the grass roots of the structure. The model does not spell out where the distinctions between senior, middle and junior management are placed. Yet it is essential the divisions are understood to determine the levels at which decisions can be taken. Failure to understand invariably means managers are paying attention to matters their juniors, or seniors, should be controlling.

The lines of communication do not support the information necessary for all levels of management to be effective. It would be a full time job for anyone to simply absorb all the information of many sorts generated by most organisations, the exact nature of each job done, warnings of future problems, plans for future policy, present instructions. Where these go, how they are processed, what action is taken, is not according to the model. An organisation is a mass of communication systems. By studying them, insight can be gained into the structure. This is not really a job for the eager manager, it involves often a knowledge of data processing, inflow and retrieval systems. But any manager can test where he sends his communication and where he receives it from, who takes action on it, and what that action is, where the effective decisions are made. He will usually find to represent what actually happens in his organisation would require so many lines on the model it would be unreadable.

None of the diagrams show the distinction between line and staff, except under the general heading of administration. Territorial and functional commanders have responsibility for staff functions. Nor does the traditional model show the disposition of materials and equipment. It shows people, but people work with materials and equipment.

The formal plan concentrates on authority and responsibility, it does not show the whole structure of the organisation, or whether it works. It shows areas and points of conflict, it may even indicate where the structure needs shoring up. The model is useful for managers trying to understand their organisation or build a new one though care is needed; too much can be read into it which simply does not happen that way, the flow of work for instance in many organisations does not follow the lines of the model, it requires only a moment's thought to see why it would not be performed speedily or efficiently if it did. There are limitations on what structure models can show. Trying to bend the organisation to match the model is tried from time to time. It has never yet succeeded.

Organisations are people, they and not the plans or models make organisations function. Good human relations management attempts to give people a sense of identity, status, achievement and participation which they can identify with objectives of the organisation. A well-designed structure may cause this to happen naturally, most will need some prompting, inevitably this will sometimes mean compromise. When problems do arise, they may be easier solved if some thought is given to the structure as well as to the people. Bad design can leave the world's best racing driver stationary.

People accept, or can be trained to accept, the duties and

constraints which membership of the organisation implies. What an organisation does will condition what it is. The police service is a good example, the characteristic is so clear that much of what it is can be understood by those outside it. Codes of discipline, patterns of behaviour and other demands made upon policemen are accepted as necessary for the organisation to attain its objectives. Yet individual organisations have a personality of their own. Different police forces, identically structured, will be different, not just in name, in a very real sense to those connected with it. The personality of the management, the degree of formality, the quality of the training, the effectiveness of the communication, the amount of public criticism, the zeal with which it seeks its objectives all fashion this identity in the same way that everyone has a nose, mouth, eyes and ears, yet looks very different. This applies to the groups within the organisation, different territorial divisions have different personalities, which may at first prove confusing to those people transferred into it; functional groups have their own characteristics. None of them can be gleaned from studying the formal organisational structure.

It is believed by some people that while there are several theories, little is known in fact about organisations, the way they function, the exact manner in which the corporate identity is formed. One method of shedding some light is by observing the interaction of the groups and sub groups. All groupings to some extent set up artificial relationships between the different functions of the organisation and the people who have to work within the boundaries. A uniform patrol constable's functions spread across those of traffic and C.I.D., the divisional administration sergeant's spreads over most functions in the division, in both line and staff. Though the relationships at this level are face-to-face where personality becomes important, the role each plays will reflect his instructions, the relationships with the same and other groups at different stages in the chain of command and at different locations within the organisation, and the sense of identification he feels with the enterprise he works in.

It is not uncommon for groups to create their own rules or ignore the formal ones where it will enhance their status power or prestige. This will lead to lack of cooperation, problems of coordination and often, inefficiency. The divisional administration will want to keep formal records, the busy detective sergeant will want an issue of pencils without, what he considers the rigmarole of, certified indents and proper receipts. Whether the detective sergeant gets pencils will depend, though he may say it is just stupidity, upon the flexibility of the groups, which conform to whose rules, how far they will compromise, whether this is because they recognise each other's problems or are forced by higher authority into protesting cooperation while looking over their shoulders for further areas of non-cooperation.

Stated starkly, and over-simplified, the problems caused by the interaction of groups, the stresses they place on their numbers who need to have one foot in each camp or continually cross boundaries, seem obvious. Where such conflicts are likely to occur is predictable to most active managers; diagnosing the many forms they take is not so easy.

There is another boundary in many organisations, the customer. Stress is caused to those in direct contact with the public when the structure or functions of the organisation cannot match the expectations of the customer, a common enough situation in operational police work. The public cannot be ignored, so they become another group whose interaction may have to be considered. Complaints of bad service, over-exercise of authority will have some effect; there are those who believe they get better service when the theft of their lawn mower is investigated by a detective instead of the neighbourhood bobby; others will seek out the senior rank at an accident because they believe he will answer the questions and deal with the incidents more effectively, though those less senior may doubt it.

Main groupings will usually be vertical, though some are horizontal. Representative organisations like the Police Federation are grouped horizontally. Interaction between horizontal and vertical groups should work for the effective functioning of the organisation, although there is ample evidence that in some organisations the opposite is true. People are placed in difficult positions when the vertical and horizontal groups they belong in are in opposition.

Every organisation has informal groups, they react in the same manner as the formal groups, producing stress and role conflict for their members. No manager should overlook them.

Organisations are made up of many different systems: in manufacturing, for instance, there will be one for acquiring raw materials, one for storing and issuing them, maybe several for producing goods. There are also systems for personnel—one for recruiting, one for training, one for assessment and appraisal. These systems overlap in many areas, they are related to others to achieve the organisation's aims, and they transcend the normal divisions within the traditional structure. By analysing the systems within an organisation, a great deal of light can be shed on how it in fact operates as opposed to how people think it operates. This is not a job for the practical manager at the grass roots, but if the systems of which he is part are ineffectual, it may be his job to promote a review of them, and in a complicated organisation with many interacting systems, the review of one necessarily means the review of others.

A systems approach to organisations recognises that systems are people, and people who have rights such as the right to question, the right to change behaviour, the right to change the structure by agreement from within. This approach must therefore be accepted by every manager, from the shiny top brass to the tarnished first liners because a systems approach implies everyone being involved in deciding objectives and the means of achieving them. Such an approach leans towards good human relations and requires the development of first line managers to the point where they under-stand the contribution of techniques such as job satisfaction, training and appraisal, and their own part in them. It does not expect managers to be professional industrial psychologists. Pro-viding the right environment is set up and the right encouragement given, most first line managers will cope, and it will add to their job satisfaction, since they will have to be more participative in running their section.

There is no perfect model: organisations are structured and shaped through many diverse processes. None of the theories of organisations — the traditional, human relations, communication, or systems, provided a complete understanding. Each indicates points where conflict and problems may arise. Whatever point of view is taken, the activities of the first line manager remains much the same: his is the face-to-face contact with his workforce; he has to work within a structure imposed from far above his head and be answerable to both for its efficiency. In many organisations this will be an interpretative role, since it is neither desirable nor practicable to lay down too many instructions and policies in great detail. Nevertheless, there can be no substitute for a manager look-ing at his organisation critically, and deciding for himself where the stresses and strains are most likely to be felt. He can then tell whether the roots of his problems are in the organisational struc-ture or the people trying to make that structure work.

It is easy to be critical, organisations do work, and as the perfect one has not yet been devised, a manager may never eradicate conflict points, though he should work constantly to that end. The constraints of the structure must be accepted where they help towards the common good. A manager may allow himself the luxury of an occasional moan about the weaknesses of his organisation, but in the long run he will have to learn to live with them while minimising their effects on his efficiency. He should legitimately seek to change them only if he can guarantee that improvement will result to the organisation as a whole, that other functions, groups or systems will not suffer to ease the running of his department. And in a complex organisation like a police force, that is easier said than done.

Fig I

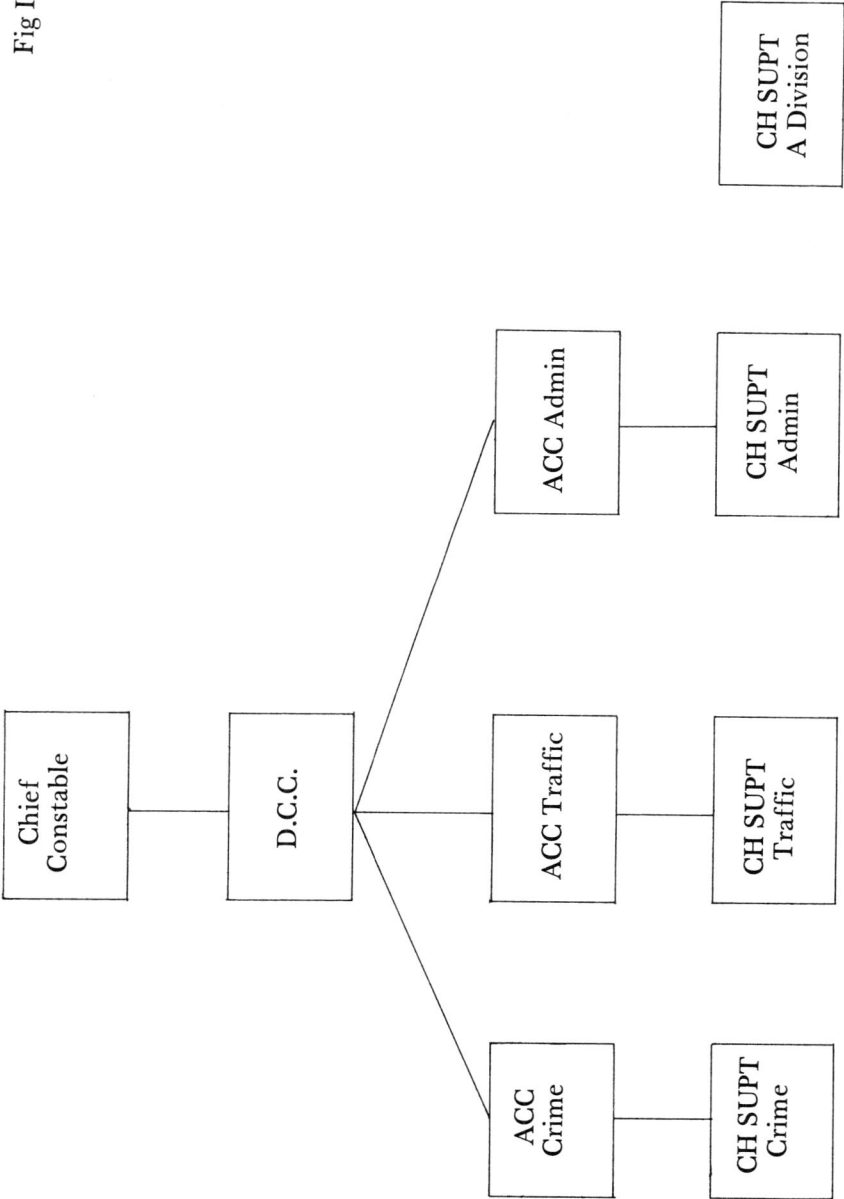

Chief Constable — D.C.C.

D.C.C. connects to: ACC Crime, ACC Traffic, ACC Admin

ACC Crime — CH SUPT Crime

ACC Traffic — CH SUPT Traffic

ACC Admin — CH SUPT Admin

CH SUPT A Division

Fig II

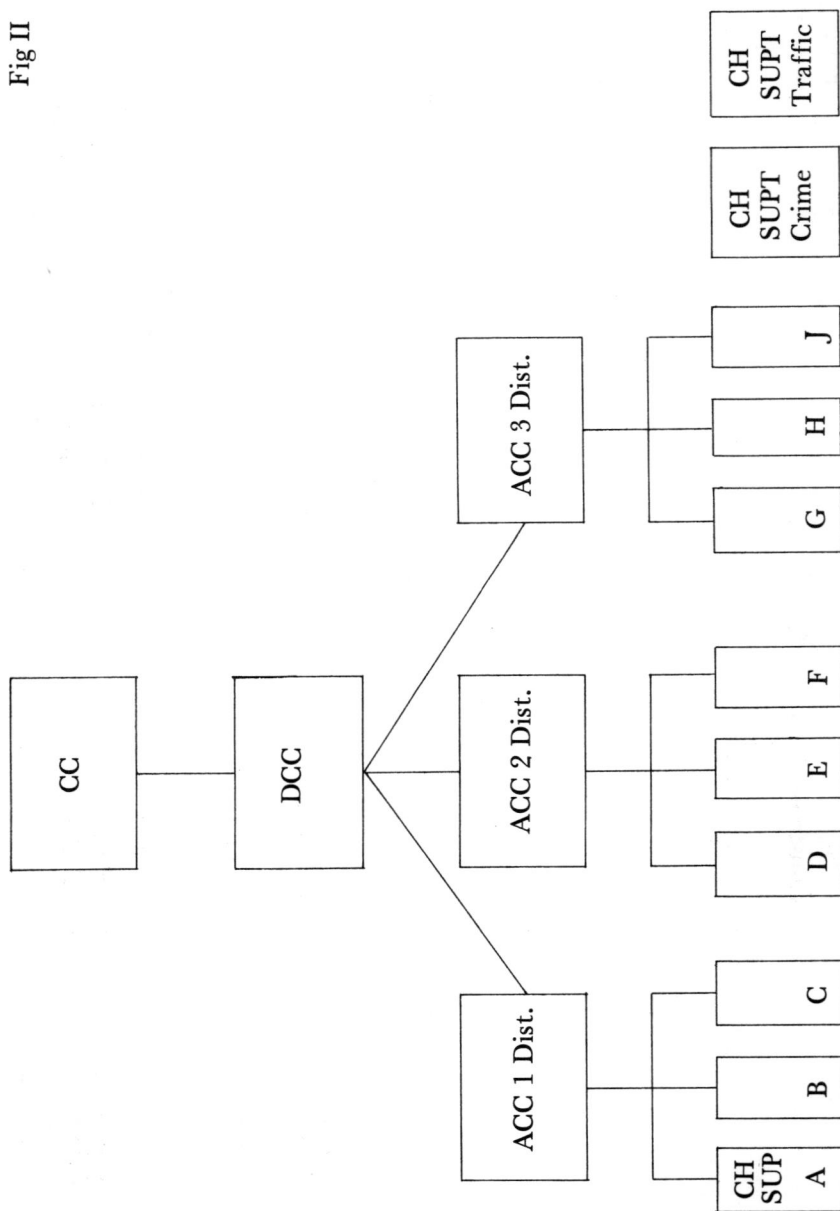

Fig III

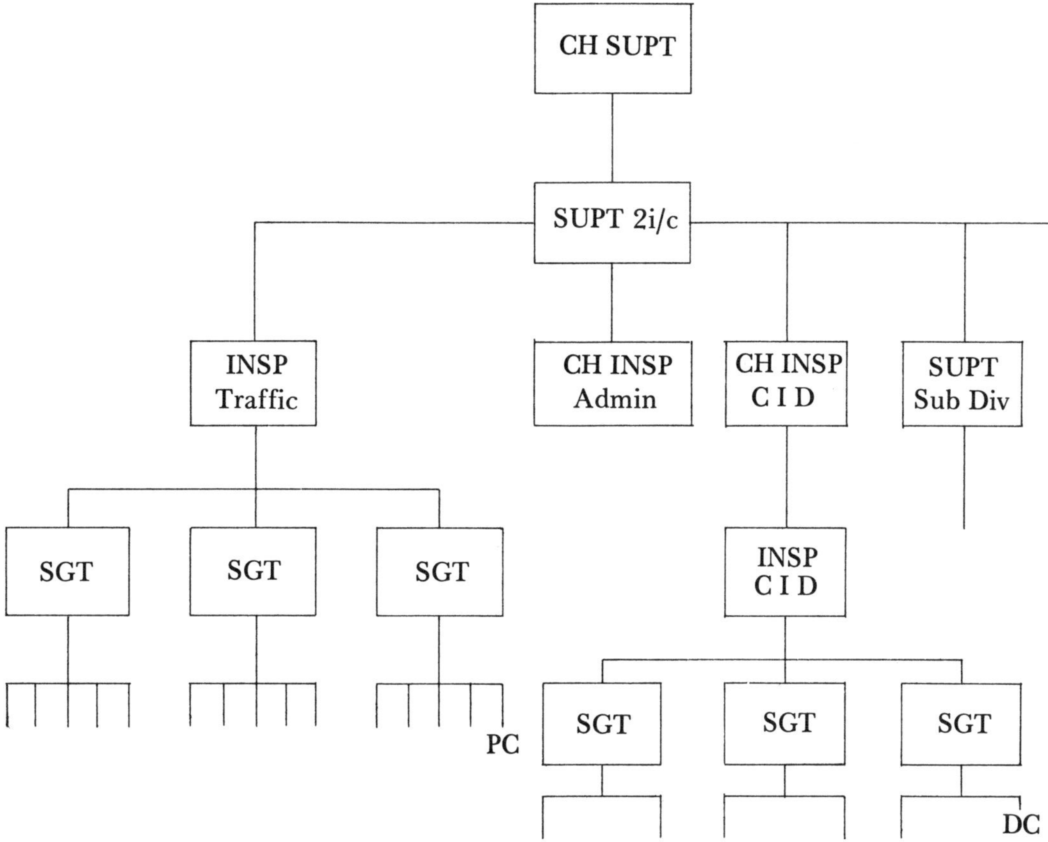

An organisational chart with the following structure:

- CH SUPT
  - SUPT 2i/c
    - INSP Traffic
      - SGT → (several vertical lines)
      - SGT → (several vertical lines)
      - SGT → PC (several vertical lines)
    - CH INSP Admin
    - CH INSP C I D
      - INSP C I D
        - SGT → (several vertical lines)
        - SGT → (several vertical lines)
        - SGT → DC (several vertical lines)
    - SUPT Sub Div
    - CH INSP Sub Div

27

2 Motivation

A HANDFUL OF RICE

Human being are a rich assortment of all the praise and blame-worthy thought and actions that man has ever put a name to, and some that defy description. The Yorkshire proverb "There's nowt so queer as fowk" sums up human behaviour, underlining the difficulties of understanding it. In many senses every human being is as unique as his fingerprints, and while this may be little help in putting people in the boxes beloved of statisticians, it provides a clue to the manager: to himself, every individual is unique.

At the same time, human behaviour in any society has points in common, it reacts to situations in broadly the same way, it has the same broad sense of values, it displays within wide margins the same attitudes. And it also has its exceptions. To manage people, it is vital to have some knowledge of what drives them, or fails to do so. A knowledge of motivation is not concerned with manipulating puppets, but understanding what goes on in the power house of the human mind, what fuels it, what clogs it up. Managers work with and through people, in many organisations people are the most valuable of all resources, yet industrial managers are heard to sigh that they wished they understood as much about the people they work with as they do about the machines. To be honest, there is no perfect blueprint, though a little knowledge, thought and interest will remove many difficulties. The success of any manager depends on the people he works with, and if he has not any idea of what they want from him and the organisation, he's as well prepared for his job as if he was planning to fell a forest with a razor blade. And there's no excuse for ignorance, managers are also people.

Like all other living things, people have certain needs, and the desire to satisfy these needs produces a drive to act in certain ways. The basic needs are those essential to life itself, air, water, food, shelter. It is no secret what happens when these needs are threatened in extreme cases like war or natural disasters, social values are discarded, the so-called law of the jungle prevails. It is not unknown for the survivors of shipwreck to resort to cannibalism to preserve life. Once any need is satisfied, the drive to act disappears, so in normal times of steady employment and state aid for the provision of essentials of life, people are not motivated by the basic drives for existence. This partly explains why pay is not a great motivating factor once it provides for basic needs, although it is important in satisfying other needs.

People have a need for security. The unknown is full of fear and apprehension. There is a need to rely on other people, wives, managers, the anonymous "them" at Headquarters. In the work situation they want to know that the sack won't come on the whim of one irrational boss, that the means of supplying the basic needs is not in jeopardy. Dismissal, or retirement, cuts people off from social contact with other people. The threat of dismissal or redundancy may motivate people for a short time, like all threats it looses effect the more it is used without being put into practice. Once the threat has been used needlessly, the effects will be counter productive.

Human beings are a mind as well as a body, both can be kicked, both can bear bruises and scars. The mind has its own needs once the bodily ones have been satisfied, and these needs provide the great driving forces which all managers should understand. It is said man is a social animal, he has social needs — few people spend their lives cut off from others by choice. Life is membership of many groups: the family, the tool room, the C.I.D, the butterfly collecting club, the regulars at the 'Pig & Whistle,' and it is through these groups that many social needs are satisfied, groupings which may be directly related to a work situation, or partly, or not at all. Strangely, it is only through association with other people that individual needs can be satisfied, everyone needs a reflection from other people to see himself. The conditions which all groups impose are the price of membership.

People also make demands upon themselves, even though they may be unaware of it; everyone has an ego demanding satisfaction. However lowly his position in life, whether through choice or not, everyone has self-respect, dignity and pride. People want to be appreciated for what they are: the tramp may not want to be prime minister, but underneath the rags and tatters he will respond to insults in the same way, to being treated as a non-person, a thing to be mocked and scorned. To the psychologist, there is little difference between the ego of the prime minister and the tramp. People need to believe in what they are doing, not just for the good of the organisation, but for their own self respect. They need to take pride in what they do; it is not unusual in this age of mass-production for people to take pride in their work, though it becomes more difficult as the age of craftsmanship slips away. Recognition of people's work must also come from others, for this fortifies the self-esteem, providing it is not misplaced. Satisfaction is easier to achieve if it is accorded by fellow workers and managers.

The main lesson for the manager in the ego need/drive area is a simple one: if people cannot gain self-respect, pride and appreciation from their work and the social conditions in which it is carried out, they will satisfy their needs elsewhere, which explains why one apparently careless and indifferent workman spent two years carefully building a model of Westminster Abbey from matchsticks.

The last, and most difficult to define, of the need/drive process is self-fulfillment, the deep inner satisfaction or contentment which comes from finding the right role in life. It is different from the ego needs, people may have those entirely satisfied, yet feel that however much their talents are praised, however high their status and self esteem, something is missing, the true vocation has not been found. This explains why millionaires leave the soft life of the penthouse to work with down-and-outs in the seamier side of town, why some policemen become priests. It also explains why some people refuse promotion which will take them away from a role in which they find fulfillment. This need/drive is difficult to recognise, many people spend their entire lives without ever knowing what they need. It is possible to satisfy the other ego needs without that for self-fulfillment ever becoming paramount.

Linked with basic psychology, there are two theories about human beings in organisational work situations. One, the traditional view, states that work is a necessary evil to be avoided where possible, and people work only because they have to.

This leads to the natural conclusion that to get people to work they have to be directed, threatened, cajoled into doing whatever tasks the organisation lays down. Human beings are a pretty sad lot, generally lacking ambition, doing the minimum necessary to keep the boss off their backs, reluctant to accept even minor responsibility. In this theory, the role of the manager becomes clear, which is strange, because the theory also applies to managers, for they are human beings.

The second theory says that work is a natural activity, as natural as rest and play. If people can see the point of what they are doing, they are capable of a high degree of self control and initiative. The satisfaction of not only the basic needs, but also the ego needs are in themselves rewards which people seek from work. Under the right conditions the average person seeks responsibility; imagination, ingenuity and creativity are widely distributed throughout the working population, they are not the gifts of a few, and these can be directed to and identified with the organisational objectives. In this theory the role of the manager also becomes clear, and it should be more acceptable, because it, too, applies to managers. Of course, there are people who fit the first theory, those who need the carrot and the stick. The gravest mistake for managers is to believe that everyone fits that theory, for it applies to no more than 20% of the working population. The second theory, which applies to 8 out of every 10 you manage, points the benefits to the manager if he can harness the potential to the organisation. But it is potential, it needs the right conditions in which it can be transformed to action. It is the manager who creates those conditions.

There is another difficulty: though the need/drives are present in everyone, their strength varies in individuals. Some are dominant at certain times, disappearing when satisfied only to reappear when the satisfaction has worn thin. Thus promotion will satisfy the need only temporarily where status and recognition in this visible form are dominant. But people are realistic about their drives, even if subconsciously; the strong ones are those they think will produce the desired results. No one will harness energy and effort to things they know are beyond their reach — even though the need remains unsatisfied, they will transfer to other ways of satisfying it — a reason why exhortations to this and that so often fall on deaf ears. Some needs, like obvious smooth running success, appear relative to age, they are often more keenly sought by the young and hence the drives will be stronger; in later life realism becomes more apparent, the needs more suited to circumstance and ability, and the drives related more directly to them; as people grow older the ego sometimes becomes less agressive. The only answer to these problems is knowledge of the people you work with, to try and understand them and their driving forces. It is no use asking them — they probably cannot express it in terms which make much sense, the ego needs come from deep inside the mind; few people can explain exactly what they want or why they do things, in a way understandable to anyone except psychologists.

Before you close the book in frustration, think back over your career. What has given you the most satisfaction, which incidents made you feel proud, respected, useful? What caused you the most upset, frustration and dissatisfaction? To what extent were these caused by your managers? It is predictable that your answers to the first question are the exercise of responsibility, recognition from others, a sense of achievement, a status and identity within the job, the interesting jobs you were involved in, the comradeship of working with other people. It is equally predictable that your answers to the second question will include lack of respect, lack of consideration for you as an individual, frustrating things which seemed to have no point, lack of interest in the tasks you were doing, never being asked for an opinion, having suggestions dismissed without the slightest consideration. Those things in the first answer satisfied your need/drives, those in the second offended or ignored them. In answering the questions you have determined motivating and de-motivating factors. To repeat, managers are people working with people, not biologists observing a different form of life such as snails. In general, what affects managers also affects others in the same way.

If some managers are asked why people work, the immediate response will be about money. The fact that everyone goes to work to earn the wherewithall to pay for the things they want in life cannot be denied. Those same managers if asked whether money provides the constant motivation to do the job at a peak of efficiency will be more hesitant, for they know there are highly-paid industries which do not have highly-motivated workforces if labour relations are anything to go by. However, like it or not, we live in a society which places high regard on physical possessions, motor cars, stereos and deep freezes. These possessions can accord status, not only in work situations, but socially. It is tempting to dismiss them scornfully, yet they can be important, and as no one can divorce social standing from their working life entirely, pay has some effect in providing a motivating force for more than the basic needs. If every house in the street has a car outside except the policeman's the demotivating force of pay is obvious, particularly in a job which traditionally makes demands not only on the man, but on his whole family. This is not to disregard a sense of vocation, simply a warning that vocation is not the paper to cover all the cracks. Rates for the job are not within the power of police managers to negotiate, nevertheless, their effects should be understood, if only to avoid de-motivation by demanding more work because, in the manager's opinion, people are paid too much already, or the not-too-rare attitude that the higher the pay the less the manager needs to be concerned with individuals.

Status is usually reflected in badges of rank, titles, where people eat, where they park their cars, where they wash their hands. Status is attractive because it is individual, an open display of approval before the eyes of colleagues and social contacts outside work. One person's status may affect the rest of their group, it is not just Mrs Smith, it is the managing director's wife, not just a sergeant, a detective sergeant. Indeed, one way of establishing a stranger's standing in the social order is asking about his job; some have status, some don't. There is a lot of silliness about formal status, the size of desk, the colour and number of telephones, but no manager should underestimate it, to some people it is important, and care should be taken if the outward show is to be reduced. In one firm an up-and-coming executive had been promoted to a job which had been secretly downgraded. As he sat at his desk on his first morning, in came a janitor and trimmed six inches of the carpet, because the area of carpet was determined by status. The new man pretended to laugh it off, though the laughter was hollow at a visible sign of how the organisation valued him, and at a time when he could have been highly charged towards the company's aims because of his promotion. Status is not usually thought about in relation to menial tasks like cleaning. In small concerns, the cleaner is often someone the other workpeople see leaving as they are arriving, and arriving as they are leaving. The manager decided that the minor inconveniences of cleaning being done at the same time as production could be tolerated, and he changed the cleaner's hours, with her consent, to coincide with the rest of the workers. Soon Mrs Mopp was truly identified as one of the workforce, people knew her name and she knew theirs. The workroom was tidier, people were more careful because they knew who was cleaning up after them, and if they weren't Mrs Mopp's status reminded them. Accidents through material being carelessly placed diminished, production improved through better order in the workroom. Altering her hours of work gave her status, acceptance within the social group of other workers reinforced it. Mrs Mopp benefited, the company benefited.

Promotion is the most obvious sign of a change in formal status, and whilst it may be beyond the power of many managers to promote, it is within the power of all to recommend for promotion. Formal status may also be accorded by transfer to other departments, other jobs where the rank does not change, but the responsibility does. There are other areas of status within the working group, which are granted as much by the group as by the manager. If a man is better at something than others, perhaps questioning suspects, that will give him status. Senior constables have status based on their experience, any police manager knows what to expect if he treats them like probationers. Whatever status people seek, either formal or informal, it is usually tied to responsibility, direct or assumed. That responsibility may be getting on with the job without the usual supervision. People respond to being trusted to make decisions, or entrusted with some area of work for which they are responsible. It is proven fact that many people have been motivated by a sense of responsibility who have previously taken a casual attitude.

Status satisfies the ego needs, it provides a place within the social groupings, which are the main informal source of control. Every manager should encourage people to achieve informal status, even though formal status is beyond his power to increase. He can encourage them to get involved, he can avoid breaking up informal groups unnecessarily, he can provide training to develop the skills and knowledge which accord status. People have a need for it, even though status is not a word they themselves would use.

There is one thing within the power of every manager which has been proved time and time again to be a good motivator. Praise. This useful fuel, is cheap, gives a high return and yet seems to be ignored on many occasions. It is a sad fact that rebukes are given out far more often than praise; are your people really that bad, or is it you, the manager, that is bad? Praise for a job well done satisfies the ego, and if given publicly may promote status and satisfy the social need for acceptance. Disapproval has the opposite effect, it irritates the ego, and indifference is the worst of all, that denies the personality. A simple pat on the back costs nothing, and if given at the time will be worth the handwritten scroll three months later. Praise must be sincere, it must not be forced or given when it has not been deserved. Insincerity, and other people can recognise it as readily as managers, only meets with contempt.

Praise is a form of recognition, people like to have their efforts recognised, for one thing it distinguishes them from others, the ego can be competitively demanding.

People appreciate recognition of the special skills or attributes they bring to their job. There's many a manager got a hard task done with enthusiasm because he gave recognition to those who came out of it well. So policemen will deal with appalling accidents in atrocious weather, face dangers in making difficult arrests because they are confident that their efforts will receive recognition. And that goes for ideas as well, managers have never had the sole publishing rights on bright ideas, which certainly won't be put forward if it is felt the rightful recognition goes elsewhere. Any manager who passes off one as his own is unlikely to get a second chance to do the same. And who knows? The fellow whose idea you pinched may be your boss one day.

Praise and recognition satisfies the ego need for achievement. It can be satisfied without them, after all men know when they have done a good job, but praise and recognition underline it. This applies to all activities, not only those that reach the newspapers; the sense of achievement in completing a difficult report is just as real to the man who has written it as that felt in making an arrest. Without a sense of achievement, any job becomes purposeless, interest in it evaporates. All jobs have their share of routine, policemen are luckier than most in the variety of their work, but the out-of-the ordinary does occur. That out-of-the ordinary may be nothing more than someone else's routine. To tackle a job never attempted before, to see it through successfully can give satisfaction and pride, together with standing in the social group.

However lowly in the organisation, everyone has his pride and self-respect. To him everyone is special, different, unique, and the most individual thing about him is his name. Numbers may be acceptable shorthand in documents or for quick identification, not to a person's face, for that denies the individuality. A man may be justly proud of his skill, perhaps in driving a powerful car safely at high speed when the situation demands; however much that skill is possessed by others, it is still a source of pride to the man who has the ability to exercise it. All men have skills and knowledge in which they take pride, even though they may be widely distributed through the organisation. They are important to those who possess them, and they are important to the organisation even if they do appear somewhat ordinary. Don't under-rate skills or knowledge, pride is easily injured, the ego slighted.

Equally, self-respect is easily affronted. One of the sad facts about the whole motivation de-motivation business is that it happens whatever the manager's real intentions. Acting exclusively on the mind, there's been as much harm done by casual comments and unintended sarcasm as by unfair criticism, failure to recognise talents, lack of recognition of effort, indifference to status, direct and indirect attacks on dignity and self esteem. All lower people in the standing of those they live and work among, all fail to satisfy the ego needs of the individual. The ego need/drive is a tender plant, if the soil in which it is rooted lacks the right nutrients it will grow stunted, bear little fruit, and may even wither away. Self-respect is vital to everyone, including managers. It is best promoted by consideration for people as individuals, for their feelings as well as their wishes. It is not granting every whim and fancy. Changes of duty have to be made, rest days have to be cancelled. People accept these more readily if they can see why they are necessary, if they feel that they have been considered instead of being dismissed with other unimportant trivia "They're here to do what they're told, the job must come first" is from the book of the disciples of the first theory.

A young policewoman of only a few months service asked for

time off on a Saturday, the first request of a personal nature she'd ever made. Saturdays are traditionally the busiest days of the week in the police service. Saturdays are also the traditional day for weddings. The policewoman's request was refused on the grounds that anything might happen, the job must go on, everyone might be needed. She accepted that the job must go on, what she could not see was how her absence would make it stop. She went to the wedding, she did not have to explain her presence there to the sergeant, she'd already resigned because she found the rules too inflexible, which is another way of saying no one considered her needs as a person, her status and self-respect within her family group. And all the forecasts about her agreed she had the makings of a fine policewoman. Motivation needs the personal touch, personal contact, effort and thought. The higher up the organisational chain the manager climbs, the wider the responsibilities, the more claims upon his time. Everyone can set a pattern of motivation with his immediate subordinates. The telephone is a handy instrument, particularly if it's raining. It does not increase the self-esteem of men on detached beats and out-stations when you ring them up because you can never find the time to visit them.

People have problems connected with their home life, sickness in the family, ageing parents to care for, financial worries, disputes with neighbours. They don't shut them out of their minds when they walk into the police station. To say it shouldn't be so is idealism, managers deal with people as they are. In many cases there will be nothing that the manager can do about the problem itself except show understanding and consideration, perhaps by the rearrangement of duties, perhaps by advice. However trivial the problem may seem to you the manager, to the person wrestling with it, it's important. There's many a domestic dispute settled officially by action which amounts to nothing more than lending a sympathetic ear. If that is refused to one of the manager's own people, then it will be construed as a lack of interest in the individual. Any organisation should be big enough to cope with its objectives and discharge its human responsibilities as well.

Of course there are full-time Welfare Officers with more time, and maybe skill, than managers. Refer your people's problems to them by all means, but still show concern, interest, compassion, avoid the impression that you're passing them off because it's the easiest way out. If your help is still required, you'll be told. Make sure that your people know why you refer them to the Welfare Officer, that it is in their best interests, that it is the best way of helping them. No one likes to be ignored, or feel that he and his problems are unimportant, however much you may feel they are the authors of their own downfall or that a simple solution stares them in the face.

Promotion has been mentioned several times as a motivating force, it is an obvious incentive, giving individuals a recognisable target. It goes without saying that every manager should train his subordinates and take positive steps to ensure promotion for those who are ready. However, promotion is not available to everyone, not everyone can be a Chief, there must be Indians too. Most people can bear this disappointment if they receive encouragement to persevere. And encouragement is not false promises. What people cannot bear is a manager who does not use the career structure to push his people on becasue he does not want to loose the good ones, the ones on whose efforts his success depends.

You will have gathered by this time that leadership is the most important motivator, and therefore bad leadership the greatest de-motivator, because it is through managers and leaders that organisations are personalised to satisfy the human needs of those within it. Those higher up the chain have a part to play, but it is the immediate managers who have the star part. A manager who is finding difficulty in satisfying his own needs because his boss is inconsiderate and the rest, is unlikely to spend much time motivating his own subordinates if he gets too wrapped up in his own problems. There is a chain of motivation, hence the not-quite-worn-out saying that if things are alright at the top, they are likely to be at the bottom. It helps to go back to the two theories of work. If you accept the first, the easier for the manager to apply because it only needs a loud voice, motivation is difficult. The second theory assumes not only that people have potential, but that they are wanting to contribute. Bad motivation prevents the second theory from being proved or disproved.

The main problem of motivation is to give freedom while retaining control. There are ways of achieving this, delegation with proper feedback for instance. Suffice it here to say that motivation is not just concerned with making people content through staisfying their human needs; it is satisfying those needs through achieving the objectives of the organisation. They may not always coincide; they will to a greater degree if thought is given by managers to both. The essential base is the establishment of a relationship based on trust between subordinates and manager in which they and their unique qualities are recognised and used. Such relationships are a delicate balance between familiarity and aloofness. Every manager has to make his own decision where he strikes this balance, depending on his personality and those of his subordinates. Whichever way he tackles it, he must display confidence in what he is doing if he is to maintain other people's. Outward displays of confidence are important, however much the butterflies may be zooming round the abdomen. Nothing is gained by any manager parading his doubts. If he's uncertain of himself he creates a sense of insecurity, it is expecting too much for others to feel certain, for he's in charge.

No manager can be a good guy all the time, mistakes will be made, people will let him down, fail in the responsibilities he entrusted to them. Then he must have the courage to assign blame. It is the only way to avoid repetition of the mistakes and encourage responsibility, not only to the manager but to the rest of the working group and the organisation. People expect to be told when they have done wrong, it is the manner in which they are told which will motivate them and their colleagues, or not. The essence is telling him what he has done wrong in a manner which preserves his dignity, status and self respect, never a "must try harder" session in which previous sins are catalogued as a penance for the offender. If others in the group know that errors are being made and the manager has not the courage to do anything about it, is that a basis on which to build understanding and trust.

It may at first sight seem strange to regard discipline as a motivating factor based on fear, not of physical harm, few autocrats order forty lashes these days, but the psychological harm which affects the ego, the reverse of praise. A scowl of displeasure can be more effective than a long-winded formal report. It is your acceptance which is temporarily denied, your disapproval because he is not living up to your expectations can be a spur for better things.

The remedy is in his own hands. Providing discipline is fair, tempered with justice and mercy, it does motivate.

There are two contradictory assumptions which managers must make if they are to motivate successfully. One is that other people are like them with ego/needs about pride and self esteem. The sticks and stones which hurt you will hurt them. Feel for others as you feel for yourself. The other assumption is that other people need not be like you in their ego/needs concerned with satisfaction and personality. If you the manager are self-sufficient, needing little reassurance from others, don't assume everyone else is the same. If you feel a sense of being unfulfilled, there's always something else you should have done to really deserve the praise you've received, don't assume others are the same. Don't think people always want for themselves what you want for them, or what is interesting to you will be the passion of their lives.

So motivation provides all the answers? No. It is beyond human ability to always avoid denting people's egos, but motivation will provide the framework in which the dents are quickly smoothed out. If you know how to turn people on, you know how to turn people off. You can be an energetic thrusting manager and take your people with you if you have the knowledge, courage and humanity to treat people as people with all their vices and virtues. It is their resourcefulness, drive and energy which fuels you to get where you are going, and they'll enjoy the journey as well. Motivation will open the fuel lines, never forget you have the power to shut them off completely if you don't understand the complicated machinery you're using.

3 Leadership

FALL IN AND FOLLOW ME

There are many approaches to leadership — a favourite lists the supposed qualities of the Wellingtons and Napoleons — leaving lesser mortals acutely aware of their own inadequacies. To those who aspire to such dizzy heights, the only word of caution is that the attributes of heroes and villains are much the same: it is the objective to which they use them that determines history's assessment. Some other approaches revolve around personality, though the relationship between it and leadership is not fixed; good guys can be bad leaders and bad guys good leaders — the test is how he leads not what he is. So, you can beat the wife, get drunk every night and flutter your pay on the horses and still be a good leader, just as you can go to church regularly, be a model of family propriety, on the committees of a dozen worthy causes, and be an absolute failure as a leader.

Other approaches look at the balance every leader holds between what he has to get done, and the people through who he has to do it. Some hold the balance should tilt one way, some another, though each agrees that people cannot be ignored. Every theory has its virtues, and each has its critics — equally learned and scientific as the theorists who propounded it. Each theory is directed principally towards top management, the Generals, the Industrialists, the Chief Constables. The higher up the organisation, the weightier the responsibilities, but there is also more freedom to choose the tools for the job, more chances to change the rules — and it is not unknown at that level to change the nature of the game — more opportunity to deflect the inevitable criticism on anyone who attempts leadership.

Nearer ground level there is little room for manoeuvre: the tools and the system are handed to the manager and he has to get on with the job, a man within an organisation managing other people within it, and none of them can change the rules very much. Yet it is with those tools and that system, playing within the rules, that a manager has to be an effective leader.

Every manager in the police is a volunteer — they accept the responsibilities when they accept promotion. No one made you volunteer, nor were you dragged protesting in chains as the accolade was bestowed. And if you want to step down from the job, you know there are ten men waiting to grab it from you tomorrow. The responsibility is that the leadership of small groups such as a section, must be as effective as the leadership of larger groups, otherwise any organisation grinds to a halt and the Chief's job becomes impossible, even for a Saint.

Once over the first flush of pride, perhaps you feel you were never trained for the job before you were promoted, never held even acting rank officially or unofficially: it is something the police service does not do much about until after the event. But the fact you were promoted at all is proof of somebody's faith in your leadership potential and sufficient personality to develop it, despite the folklore surrounding promotion boards. And you already have plenty of examples to study, you have your own ideas about the Sergeants and Inspectors you have worked with. Why would men do anything for Sergeant So-and-so, when all he seemed to do was play hell with them? Why was Inspector Whatsisname so ineffective, even though the poor chap obviously tried so hard? It is worth considering, for policemen do not change, and if you got het up at being left on point duty in the pouring rain because someone forgot to tell you the road had been cleared, so will the fellow *you* forget to tell.

Police managers, like those in industry, are imposed upon a group in the sense that the group has no say in the matter. Often, taking up your command is the first time you have seen them, although no doubt the grapevine will have been at work in both directions. If you are going to lead successfully, you must first gain their respect, confidence and acceptance, not by being mates together, but by leading. If you do not, the group will throw up its own leader: he will have authority but responsibility to no one, as anyone can vouch who has seen the devastating effect of a skilled 'canteen lawyer.' This does not mean, set out to be popular — you are doomed to failure. It is a hard fact of life that stripes on your arm make old colleagues see you differently, as you will see them in time. Old Charlie, whom you secretly admired for pulling the wool over the Sergeant's eyes will now be trying to pull it over your's. And sooner or later you will have to make a decision crucial to the job but unpopular with the group, like dropping late turn men back to nights. What price popularity then?

Your acceptability will depend upon your approach; whether it is positive, assessing and dealing with situations without waiting for instructions; whether you consider your men, their feelings, whether you use their talents and give them credit for it; whether you explain what is happening and how it affects them and you; whether you develop their professional expertise so they can see for themselves they are making progress; whether you build a team they are proud to be part of, even if they would not dream of telling you — in short if they are satisfied in what they are doing and can see the purpose in it; or whether it is negative, relying on Standing Orders and the Discipline Regulations; whether you fail to give instructions and then lay the blame everywhere except upon yourself; whether you're interested in other people's opinions and allow them to express them; whether you ignore their personalities so they think any ten men would be all the same to you, whether you take the trouble to explain what you're doing, or whether you pursue your own interests at the expense of everyone else.

If you have just done a quick mental check and come to the conclusion you are a positive sort of chap, consider one of the temptations in assessing your own leadership is to be sincere and accurate, and hopelessly wrong. That's why all those grids and boxes should be treated with suspicion — no one can be scientifically objective about himself, it's too easy to convince yourself you are in the right box when in truth you should be half a dozen below. The Inspector who said he thought at one time he lacked humility but now he was almost perfect, honestly thought he was being objective. Place yourself in your subordinates' shoes: how would they describe you? What does your boss think of the way you set about the job? Perhaps you dismiss this leadership stuff as nonsense, the application of half baked science leading only to the breakdown of discipline. Perhaps you sincerely believe that no Sergeant or Inspector has enough authority to decide his own pattern, the organisation doesn't let him, he cannot consult, he cannot decide, he cannot even discipline properly, nor can he get his men going in what he sees the right direction, everything important is done way above his head. He might have stripes or stars, but he is just like everyone else, he does what he's told.

Certainly some of it is done upstairs — how much is left depends not only on your boss, but primarily on what you are willing to accept. Like it or not, you will promote attitudes and affect morale, you can consult both subordinates and immediate superiors, you will make many decisions which bind not only your group but the whole service; you can set objectives; you can institute your own informal training schemes; and you will discipline, even if not through formal punishments. There is no valid reason why your leadership can't equal anything in the force, even though it's carried out away from the apparent seats of power.

No leader is free from pressure on his leadership. The Chief Constable has his Police Committee and its sometimes awkward questions and the Home Office to contend with; the press, the public, and most of all, the great pressure that swells from the force he leads. Pressures from above, below, and both sides. Its nature differs, yet it comes from the same directions as the pressures on you. How you deal with that pressure from all the different directions is going to fashion your style of leadership.

The pressure from above is to get the job done efficiently, speedily in the acknowledged manner with some regard for your men and the rules of the organisation. This involves your ability to make decisions, including the unpopular and commonplace. It is not difficult to give instructions which will be carried out anyway, most policemen know the routine without being told. What counts is how you deal with the off key, the potentially damaging, the unexpected; how far you rely on precedent and the book, to what extent you expect instant obedience whatever the circumstances; when and where you use your initiative and in whose interests; whether you shirk the decisions so that none are made or pass them up because you can't make up your mind or are frightened of the consequences, or pass them down so you can plead innocence if they are wrong; whether you exceed your authority, committing your superiors to causes they cannot sustain, or refuse to accept it so someone has to do your job for you; whether you commit your subordinates to jobs in which they can't be successful, refusing to listen when they try to explain. Your superiors want you to be right most of the time; they expect you to be reasonable all the time. Your subordinates are interested in your decisions, they would like them to be clear cut and explained so they know where they stand, they do not like being fobbed off with promises to let them know which are never kept. Not unnaturally, subordinates want decisions they consider reasonable, and sometimes this means favourable. And by reasonable, subordinates means decisions which acknowledge their interests have at least been considered. Assume it has been decreed from above that time off will not be granted on nights; Constable Plod wants to attend a dinner dance with his wife; it is a sudden invitation and he does not ask until the night before believing sincerely that there are enough men to carry on without him. He, and more importantly Mrs. Plod, want an answer, there are babysitters and hairdressers to arrange. It is easy to say "sorry old chap", but you can allow it, and what are the implications of both possible answers? A man is reported threatening passers-by with a carving knife. How many men do you send, if it is true, someone could be injured? At midnight, there is no one to ask, unless you are going to get the boss out of bed. These are the sort of decisions YOU have to make each day you are on duty, and not all will satisfy both your subordinates and your senior officers. You also have to accept that you will not always be right, nor will your subordinates. You will have to tolerate mistakes made in genuine effort to do something for the service, like any other manager. It is said if you are right more often than wrong, you are not doing badly, and if everybody's right all the time, who the hell is doing the thinking round here!

This two-way pressure stretches the loyalty your superiors are entitled to expect from you as much as your subordinates. Loyalty is a concept easier to relate to individuals than organisations, to your section than the police service. Theoretically, they should be the same. In practice they conflict, stretching you on an agonising rack. Take a common example — orders are received which you know will be resented by your shift. You could ignore the orders, wrong though that would be for obvious reasons. Reverse the situation — your section wish you to put forward a suggestion about beat working that you know will be ill-received perhaps to the extent that you will be condemned for putting it forward. In each case you should explain, but the orders must be carried out, the suggestion submitted. You are under no obligation to pretend you support other people's ideas until they receive official sanction, like orders, then you must swallow your objections. It is your job to warn your superiors of consequences, to ask for information which may not be clear, to report back effects. Loyalty is earned, not accorded because of a rigid rank structure. That includes the loyalty of your boss to you. If you play fast and loose with him, how do you think your lot are going to be with you.

In your position it is easy to hide behind both superiors and subordinates, tempting sometimes to play them off against each other. Do not agree with your section then disagree when you are in front of the Superintendent. Apart from being morally dishonest, these things have an unfortunate habit of becoming public knowledge. Nor, if you have to take unpleasant steps should you pretend it is someone else's order. One Inspector prefaced his instructions so often with "The Chief Inspector says . . . " that he continued to say it months after he was made the Chief Inspector.

When you sound off about your bosses in front of subordinates, remember you are criticising the chain of command in which you are a link, thereby undermining their confidence in you. It is easy to blame "them" at Headquarters for your misfortunes, "they" do not understand, "they" do not care, "they" do not know what is going on. And "they" cannot defend themselves. Criticising "them" does not increase your acceptability or firmly associate you with subordinates, however much they may encourage your performance. If you are doing your job, there should be no sides. Your job may well be to lead in a direction someone else points, even though you disagree. Your section will not thank you for leading them up the garden path, or allowing them to wander through the flower beds, however pretty the immediate view. The repercussions will effect them as much as you. Besides, major problems in industry are caused by taking sides, by labelling people and scoring points off them, by blaming one another instead of looking for reasons. There are greenfly in the best rose gardens: arguing whose fault it is will not get rid of them, or protect the blooms.

Your superiors are looking at your ability as an organiser, planner, administrator and controller and you will do all of them despite their high sounding names. Your subordinates are more concerned with your acceptability, if you set out just to please the boss, you will be known as the boss's man, you'll be suspect, your acceptability will diminish, morale will droop. Concentrate on acceptability at any price and you'll experience difficulty in control, the job won't get done, the pressure from above will increase. For a short time you may manage to run with both hare and hounds, but in the end the conflicting pressures of the chase will leave you limp and breathless chasing your own tail, your acceptability exhausted, your effectiveness seriously in question and your loyalty in all directions discredited.

The true test of leadership is whether it achieves the objectives the organisation lays down. You will be forgiven the occasional unpalatable decision if superiors and subordinates can see the reason for it and know the situation demanded you acted a little out of character. Their assessment of your leadership won't be prejudiced by such isolated incidents, it will be based on a pattern over many situations, and if that pattern is wholesome, they may even have expected the unpalatable bit as the only reasonable answer to the problem, albeit against their interests. Acceptability need not be a barrier to efficiency, nor need it strain loyalty. There is no book blueprint, much will depend on your personality and the relative importance you place on the different aspects of the job, but these are some of the attitudes people look for in a leader.

1. *Treat people with respect.* Subordinates are not inferiors. They like to be addressed by name, just like you. Respect means showing concern for them as individuals, appreciating their talents, making some allowances for their weaknesses, allowing them to have a point of view. If you respect them, they will probably respect you.

2. *Be Polite.* There is no harm in it, there is no valid logic in supposing instructions must be given in a formal impersonal manner. There is nothing wrong with making it sound like a request, or saying please, it is only sugar on the pill, the subordinate knows he cannot refuse. Rank can never excuse rudeness.

3. *Be Honest.* In every sense of the word. You are not going to agree with everybody all the time unless you are a "yes" man, but you can disagree without making an issue from every difference of opinion. It helps if you take the trouble to explain. Acknowledge your own mistakes and take the blame. You can also apologise without losing face, discipline does not instantly disintegrate if you say "sorry". Honesty includes giving credit where it is due. You are in a privileged position to put forward other people's ideas, to push their achievements. Claim the credit once and you will never be trusted again. Be honest with assessments and appraisals, have the courage to tell a man what you think. He may not like it, he will like it a lot less if you tell him one thing and write another. Honesty really amounts to doing what you expect will be done to you.

4. *Be Impartial.* It is human nature to like some people more than others, often for no apparent reason. Keep your personal preferences to yourself, try and treat everyone the same. Do not give favours, do not look for whipping boys. Obvious, you will say, but you would not be the first sergeant to do it and be the only man on the section not to notice. It is a sad fact of life that we appreciate most those who agree with us, even though they

are wrong as well.

5. *Exercise Restraint.* You will fall out with the wife, trip over the station cat, fail to get the promotion you know you deserve and arrive some days feeling bloody-minded. It is not the fault of the section so do not take it out on them. They will not know about your private problems or be aware of the stresses of your job, they have enough to do coping with their own, do not put yours on their shoulders. One unreasonable irrational hour can wipe out a lot of what you have taken months to achieve. "I would not dream of it". Not deliberately, perhaps, yet it is one of the things all people do if they do not watch themselves. And if you are one of those who blast ten thousand feet up with little provocation, have a long countdown first. You may feel better for your trip, your subordinates won't, they will just keep out of your way.

6. *Be Approachable.* You do not have to be solemn to be serious. A smile and a willingness to listen more than compensates for a face which does not appear welcoming. Being approachable encourages free speech, it eases constructive communication. You will not get ideas, advice or warnings, nor hear of grievances and complaints if you are haughty and distant. You can often put a little grievance right before it becomes important — there is more than one strike been caused by a petty irritation that the manager would have corrected instantly had he known about it. Being un-approachable he did not, and it festered until the final effect had no relation to the cause. Saying "no one told me" does not absolve you from responsibility.

7. *Be Consistent.* Not only in your moods, snapping a fellow's head off one day will not induce him to confide in you the next, when you feel better. If you need to sulk occasionally, go away and do it in private, it is one of your privileges. A boss who blows hot and cold, turns sometimes this way sometimes that, causes suspicion, subordinates do not know how to take him, so they leave him alone. Be consistent in your demands, lay down standards and keep to them, it gives subordinates a sense of security when they know what is expected of them, nor will they complain too loudly if they fail, they will know where. Standards apply to turn-out, report writing, punctuality, anything you care to add. If you think about all you are responsible for, you control an awful lot of standards.

8. *Set an Example.* In everything. It is a hard rule, although that is why you get the extra money. Actions speak louder than words

if you slide away ten minutes early every day, so will your shift. If you cannot be bothered to clean your shoes, do not expect your section to clean theirs. You will need more than average gall to reprimand and rebuke men for doing something you do yourself. Set an example in attitudes, some jobs are boring, repetitious and routine. If you can tackle them with zest your attitude will spread, just as it will if you are a born grumbler or senior officer discrediter. Be enthusiastic and look for improvement and the raising of standards. It is the difference between doing what falls on your desk and doing what needs to be done.

9.   *Be Discreet.* You will learn things which may cause embarrassment to subordinates and superiors, show them you can keep a secret. If you feel obliged to disclose a confidence, warm people before hand and explain. They will often understand. If you are indiscreet, no one will have the confidence to tell you anything.

10.   *Do not make promises you cannot keep.* Even with the best intentions. You may fob people off, but do not promise anything it is not in your power to grant, like putting a man on traffic, if that it is your boss's prerogative — he may not do it. Confidence in you is shattered and it is your own fault. "Leave it to me" makes a subordinate believe something is going to happen, he is too disillusioned for explanations when it does not. False promises, intentional or otherwise, undermine your authority.

11.   *Be Just.* Your sense of justice is constantly monitored by the group you lead and injustice against one is injustice against all. Bear in mind that you can be too lenient, thereby not making it clear how serious you regard a situation. When it happens again, your subordinates may be genuinely surprised at the ferocity of your wrath. You can also be too harsh, this is easy enough when something has gone wrong, through the red mist you may scream for revenge. It is in times of stress that your leadership is tested, the very times that your subordinates are looking to see just how good you really are. Do not let them down and do not let yourself down — a sense of justice and perspective will help.

That list is one more than Moses received, though in its context they are just as important. They are not commandments, just observations on some of the attitudes all managers are faced with. They are not even a guarantee of success, though they will go some way towards it. If you choose to disregard them, and there may be situations where you take a deliberate decision to do so, at least you should know the likely consequences.

The sideways pressure comes from people of equal rank or

responsibility, usually in two different styles. First, operational pressures — traffic cars need observers, the CID have hot information and need men to observe. Obviously there has to be co-operation or the job would not get done, but can you fail to meet your obligations through helping others? Is it your job to fill gaps in manpower and equipment from your slender resources (when has anyone had enough of both), particularly if a bit of foresight and planning should have been used? Specialists tend to regard themselves as special, their job is always more important then anyone else's. If you do not set an example of co-operation, your section will not co-operate when they ought: if you are willing to assist, the demands may increase, your section will resent doing what they consider other people's work, you will affect dignity, morale will dip. Refusal may be in the best interests of the section, but not in the general interest of the division. Sorry, there is no book answer, except a reminder to consider all the angles before you decide.

The other sideways pressure comes from closer colleagues. "Don't rock the boat". "Don't try anything new". There is a belief that anyone displaying energy and resourcefulness shows up his colleagues, and it is not unknown for quiet words to be said to calm him down. The belief is mistaken, and if you are on the right lines, do not get sidetracked into some vacant siding. Of course you are different, so are we all. From that simple fact stems all the joys and all the tribulations of working with people. Colleagues may, from time to time, enlist support in petty squabbles among themselves. The issue may be emotional, loaded with rights and wrongs, there will be great appeals to principle, it will be put so that refusal to join the cause seems churlish. You may even have private sympathies. It requires moral courage to pursue what you know to be right, to stand aside from what you sense to be wrong, and remain cordial.

The points made above about relationships with subordinates apply equally to other managers. There is just one more to add — if you have become involved with someone else's section, tell him what you have done, do not leave him to find out from someone else. Apart from being courteous, it will prevent him getting a distorted tale, particularly if you have been a little tough.

Nothing said above conflicts with the demands made upon you by your superiors, yet all will go a long way towards making you acceptable with your group. Do not think it is all going to happen the first time you stroll into the parade room oozing charm. You will have to work at it; you will need a fair amount of moral courage, a high degree of professional competence, a liberal portion of honest endeavour and above all, a fierce determination to be a good leader, a good manager. You will need all those, yet none are beyond the scope of anyone who has been promoted, none of them depend on silver spoons in infant mouths or signs of the zodiac. Like it says in the sales talk, leadership is within your grasp if you take a little trouble to reach for it. This is not soft pussyfooting nonsense, ill-suited towards a disciplined service. So let us consider that thorny, misunderstood, bone of contention, discipline.

4 Discipline

THE WICKED WICKED WORLD

The word "discipline" comes from an old word meaning teaching or training; disciplined troops are well-trained, not those prompted perpetually by the sergeant — major's voice. Certainly discipline may involve formal punishment, but is concerned with attitudes more than deeds; it does not mean constant supervision and correction, over-attention to petty offences, endless formalities and restrictions. The best disciplined groups are the least punished, and in some respects for the manager, the easiest to work with.

It is in the nature of the policeman's task that unless the manager is going to work with him for eight hours a day, constant supervision is impossible. Policemen spend much of their working lives alone, his sergeant or inspector is rarely in the position of the platoon commander who can look along a line of trenches and see all his men. It is apparent that discipline must come from within policemen themselves, an attitude in which they will be guided more by their immediate supervisors than Force Orders or the Discipline Regulations. As leaders, sergeants and inspectors adopt positive or negative attitudes towards discipline which are reflected in their men. Negative discipline is restrictive, it concentrates on the prevention of mistakes, apportioning blame, checking, criticising, condemning. It operates mainly through fear, people avoid mistakes because of the unpleasant consequences. If negative discipline is imposed too harshly, avoidance of mistakes becomes the subordinate's main occupation, he will retreat from any situation which has no formally-approved course open to him, and there are not too many of those in the million and one jobs a policeman may be called upon to do. If men are criticised for everything they do, they won't do anything, for the result is exactly the same and it is easier.

Positive discipline acknowledges mistakes and will apportion responsibility with the object of avoiding them in future because they are unproductive. Men are not too resentful of correction in general if it is explained why it is necessary, what can be learnt from it, what course to take in future, that there may be results initiated by an officer with repercussions far along the chain of command. Once the positive attitude is fostered, communication will be established which may point out defects in training, administrative or operational systems. Well disciplined people do things right because that is the best way of doing them, not because they are terrified of errors.

The constable's notebook is checked periodically by the sergeant. If this is done only to see that margins have been ruled, refreshment times recorded, pages not torn out, the check will achieve these things — probably. The procedure gives the sergeant a golden opportunity to talk about the entries, why they are made in that fashion (it is not always obvious to young policemen), to offer advice and note difficulties not only with the notebook entries, but the incidents to which they relate. This approach may change the notebook in the probationer's eyes from just another official record to something personal in which others take an interest and he takes pride. It will conform to Force Orders because the constable wants it that way.

It is not pretended things never go wrong. The negative attitude seeks out those responsible without bothering to find out reasons. Most people know when they've made a mistake, a verbal lashing only rubs salt into an already painful wound. This situation, in which too much reprimanding is self-defeating, only causes hurt, embarrassment, makes people feel so sorry for themselves they are unwilling to learn anything from their mistakes.

Trifles may have serious consequences, grave errors none. It should be the man's actions which are considered, not repercussions no crystal ball could have foreseen. On the other hand, there are somethings which should be foreseen — the slamming of a car door has warned more than one potential prisoner.

The following are steps which can be taken to encourage a positive attitude towards discipline:
1. Look for mistakes before they happen. If you make a habit of keeping a close eye on what is going on, people will come to accept it and not think you don't trust them or are always interfering. You will see things going awry before they get serious. Preventative medicine is more painless than surgery.
2. Actions speak louder than words. If you refuse to accept your responsibilities, so will your subordinates. You are in a priviledged position, you can pass the buck down. Keep it where it belongs. If it arrives hot in your hands, don't start a chain reaction.

3. Don't assume men make mistakes deliberately. There are two sides to most questions, so always ask for an explanation before you launch into your speech. That is a privilege accorded the meanest criminal. If you reprimand before you hear an adequate explanation you will create a sense of injustice and feel foolish.

4. Be impartial, people accept criticism more readily when they know it applies equally. If some get away with it and some do not, people may think you have favourites or don't know what you're doing. Either way, they will feel slighted and won't listen to you.

5. Let your standards be known. It is your interpretation of rules and regulations which count with your team. You will cause bewilderment if you reprimand for falling short of standards they have never heard about.

6. Be firm, but be consistent. People like to know where they stand, they prefer the right bastard all the time to a sergeant who changes with the wind. Deal with each incident as it arises. It is tempting to put it off, it becomes difficult to correct something you have tolerated many times before.

7. Discuss errors and reprimand in private, or you destroy people's dignity. Only clowns want to appear foolish in public. Few incidents are so urgent that the reprimand must be then and there. Reprimands in public attract sympathy the offender does not deserve, they affect morale and undermine the leader's position.

8. Praise in public. There is nothing so dispiriting as to be told consistently when you are wrong, yet never a word when you are right. Praise fortifies morale. When it seems impossible to receive it, people stop trying to earn it.

9. Tell people what they have dong wrong. Be specific, not a general umbrella discourse of dissatisfaction. And speak about the offence, not the man, even genius has its imperfections. Do not ridicule, swear or shout, you will loose control and he will stop listening. If he is not listening and you are not telling him what is wrong, he can't be expected to remedy it.

10. Be open and honest; don't set traps or look for scapegoats. You can find out why things go wrong only if people tell you. Policemen resent subterfuge as much as anyone else; if all that is being sought is someone to hang the job on, no one will talk.

11. Listen to complaints, grievances and suggestions, they are the

key to the real situation. You may be able to do something about it, or get someone else to do it. Experience is learning from mistakes, though not everyone has to put a hand in the fire to know it burns.

The pressure on you from above is to maintain control. Discipline reinforced by rank and the authority of the organisation is one way of doing it. The pressure from below is to create an agreeable working climate. The positive approach to discipline will allow you to bear those pressures.

Not that it is suggested it will work in every case. You must decide what to pass up higher, perhaps for formal disciplinary proceedings, or a final "or else" from the Chief Superintendent. No one can advise you in every case, you must be guided by your Force Instructions. And you must also feel that you have done all you can. In considering what to pass up, you should have regard to the rest of the section. They may appear sympathetic towards a colleague heading straight for the Chief's carpet, but not if he deserves it. And they usually know. It is in the true interests of the section that disobedience and poor job performance are checked immediately. Policemen, like everyone else, want to know why one gets away with it; if he can, others will try when it suits them. Standards will gradually be lowered, second best accepted; not perhaps detectable from day to day, though over six months it is noticeable. And you are the leader. You are responsible.

Complaints against the police arouse passionate emotions. You may have to deal with them in the initial stages against your own men. They expect supporting to the hilt, that is what loyalty is all about, they say, explaining, often with truth, that the complaint is ill-founded, exaggerated or downright malicious. Your wider loyalty to the organisation should overcome personal feelings. In attempting to cover up a complaint you are being less than honest, certainly disobeying orders, and using conduct of which you would be the first to complain if it was used against you. Despite the unpleasant tensions of an investigation, the only path is the straight and narrow. You will have told suspects sincerely that they have nothing to worry about if they have done nothing wrong; it is the same for policemen. There is not a single case of a policeman disciplined on the sole evidence of an irate motorist who resented being reported for speeding. There is plenty of myth and folk lore. There are no facts.

Often a calm-rational explanation to a would-be complaint

will satisfy him. The public are somewhat ignorant of the policeman's responsibilities, though they will cooperate if told why; why policemen look in suitcases carried in the early hours of the morning by shabby men in a select piece of suburbia, that to look in the case does not mean that policemen don't know that people change digs at that time of day, or that people who tell such tales must be liars. An explanation by someone in authority, you, will smooth down ruffled feathers. Pretending through misplaced loyalty that it really is not proper to complain about the police will calm nobody down.

Treat all men the subject of a complaint as innocent until proved otherwise, though that doesn't mean looking at them through rose-coloured glasses. You should know them better than anyone. There are many pitfalls in a copper's life. outraged innoncence on their behalf helps neither, them, you nor the job.

The aspects of the positive approach to discipline are the same as the positive approach to leadership. Both will keep control, both will achieve the objectives of the organisation, both will lead to good morale.

Groups of people have an identity of their own, quite separate from the individual identities. Morale is something akin to the motivation of groups, in particular the relationships within the groups and outsiders, which may include the leader.

Every organisation has informal groups. They won't go away because they're ignored. They can be good for the health of an organisation. Any leader belongs to at least two himself. The leader can expect subordinates to obey his instructions, provided they are within the ambit of his formal authority. The leader's power comes from his position within the organisation. From this may follow the mistaken idea that because of this position, all a leader has to do is cry "Let's go chaps", and that is it, especially if Force Orders are waved when the command is given. This idea strangely persists despite all the theories and the daily experience of all who try to manage people successfully. The evidence indicates that leadership is subject to pressures from unlikely groups, who can in certain circumstances negate all the best-intentioned efforts of the leader. Yes, even in a disciplined service.

Besides bringing home the bacon, work is an activity supplying basic needs. At work there are other people with whom people identify on a personal basis, perhaps through shared interests inside or outside work, perhaps through shared activities. If you think of the people you work with, do you sit in the canteen with people you don't like if you can avoid it? Do you seek out people with whom you have nothing in common? Sharing a job cannot itself make people willingly share interests or more than go through the motions of sharing activity. People who do share interests or activities come together quite naturally into groups which will often cut across the formal groupings of the organisation, though they may also coincide. A force rugby team for instance, may have within it men of different ranks and from different departments. There is no order posting people to these groups, they form because the people in them want them to form. Within each group there will be someone to whom the rest turn for leadership, probably the person who in the opinion of the rest is most likely to further the objectives of the group, whatever they may be, the rugby enthusiasts, the gardening society, a communist cell. The authority of the leaders of these groups is personal, they have no position at all in the formal structure, they cannot rely on that to support their leadership. Their authority is by common consent of the group. As the formal organisation does not appoint informal leaders, it can't fire them either. The formal structure, certainly in some industries, has the greatest difficulty in controlling informal groups and their leaders, who can face towards the organisation — or away from it.

Turn informal groups inwards towards the job, and there is harnessed a potential for morale and motivation that will improve group performance and make the leader's task immeasureably easier. Turn the informal groups away from the job and the leader had better reach for the little pills the doctor prescribed.

If groups are to be encouraged to face in the right direction, there are one or two points about them which should be taken into account. Every group has its own sense of values, even a gang of criminals, it preserves its integrity by upholding those values; it imposes sanctions against its members when those values are ignored. Thus, the over-zealous constable who persists in reporting people for a long succession of trivial offences is more likely to be brought in check by his colleagues than his supervisor. Groups also impose sanctions against a leader or the formal structure when its values are ignored, perhaps by industrial action. There are so many avenues of non-cooperation in any organisation that sanctions present the group with no problems.

Failing to answer the "defective" radio and sickness by rota are two examples, insistence on carrying out strict though inappropriate procedures is another. These values should not cause too much conflict in the police service, except where different ranks have widely divergent views of the same situation, an argument perhaps for not getting out of touch with what is happening on the ground or in other departments.

Groups also provide status, and informal though it may be, it should not be overlooked. The formal structure promotes and transfers, it is the informal structure which accepts or rejects, and this is true of all levels and all ranks. Informal status depends upon the acceptance of values as well as acceptance of interests, and partly explains why some people make out in different branches of the service, and some do not, and why some of those branches regard themselves as superior.

Part of any social activity is keeping people informed about what is going on, particularly if they feel threatened, and groups are no exception. Informal groups use the informal communications system known as the grapevine, which relies on face to face contact between interested parties and operates at a speed which leaves the formal system gasping. The grapevine will be looked at later as a communications system in its own right — the point here is that groups are more likely to believe the grapevine than the formal systems because whilst it's not always accurate, people involved have several things in common with the originators of the information.

There are four main areas where conflict between groups and the formal structure or the leader are likely to occur. The first is resistance to change. This may threaten the group's membership, or its goals. The group has come together through interest and has a stake in maintaining the status quo. It is not unknown for protest groups to work against the changes they were calling for if that threatens the group. Resistance to change is shown by closing the ranks, by refusing to implement new ideas, and perhaps by operating sanctions. The challenges to informal groups are not always obvious to outsiders, though the reactions are. A good leader should have some idea of the real problems if his communication is working.

The second area is role conflict. Everyone has two work roles, one within the formal structure, the other informal. The time comes in even the happiest organisation when they clash. What is best for the job is not for the group, what is satisfactory for the group is not for the individual. The individual is pulled in two directions, anxious not to let colleagues down, yet unwilling to jeopardise his future prospects. This is a real strain which can produce unpredictable results. In these circumstances people clutch at straws. Role conflict explains why some people fail to live up to their potential after promotion, or in a new department or station. The leader who is aware of role conflict can sometimes help the subordinate avoid it, or at least be understanding until new values are accepted, new groups joined.

The third area is rumour, of which more anon, but again, it is based upon a common interest! People don't talk about things they're not interested in. The interest is not always maliciously inclined, when people are not interested enough to talk is the real time to worry, for as the Duke of Wellington is supposed to have said, it is when the troops are not grumbling they are really unhappy. The truth does not automatically kill rumour, it has to be the truth acceptable to the group, the truth which does not attack the sense of values and group priorities.

The last area of conflict is group delusions. Because a group thinks of an idea, because a majority believe it is good, the group thinks its goals are right even when in opposition to the formal goals. In this respect, informal groups are no different from some formal committees or individuals. The delusions provide the informal leader with moral backing, so the group will stand firm against any opposition to its goals, and if the formal leader attempts it, he will be regarded as autocratic. The only solution is tact and diplomacy. The big stick and the rule book only harden resolve in these circumstances.

It has been said that the formal and informal structures should work together like the blades of a pair of scissors, for while there is little doubt that informal groups may pose serious problems to formal leaders, they have advantages as well. If the leader is at odds with his group, he cannot turn in the standard of performance expected. It is up to him to create the team or group spirit and turn it towards the job, and if he is successful the standard of performance will be high. Morale is something that has to be fostered, nurtured like a young plant. There will inevitably be conflicts, it will not happen overnight. Then, it's never been suggested that effective leadership was easy.

Through their goals, groups supply a sense of purpose for many people, they are a natural environment. Everyone has seen sections without purposes, with apparently little more to achieve than the quick passage of their eight hours. Or that sense of purpose may be opposition to the leader. The maintenance men in a large factory resented the manager taking his coat off and doing their

work, particularly as his skills were rusty. They formed an anti —
boss society with written rules, and enforced membership by informal sanctions. It was to this group that the foremen went with
their problems for it determined priorities. The boss knew morale
was high, though he couldn't understand why his overall planning
went consistently wrong, why production was perpetually affected
by minor breakdowns, in short why he could not manage. He still
did not know when he was sacked. One police section went sea
fishing together every month. Morale was high, the league table of
catches was read in preference to Criminal Intelligence reports.
Although they worked well at routine jobs, the inspector could
not improve their performance after he innocently changed a few
fishing rest days. Trivial perhaps, but still important to the leader.
The moral about morale is simple: morale can be high and the job
done badly unless that morale arises essentially in relation to the
job and the formal structure.

It is essential that formal and informal goals coincide as much as
possible, a leader who ignores either does so at his peril.

The goal, or to borrow a phrase from the criminal law, the
common purpose, must have some relevance to the group. "The
War against Crime", "Maintaining the Queen's Peace" sound noble
on the public platform, they are too wide and woolly to lift
morale. Arresting a thief helps both these causes, it may be insig-
nificant to an individual policeman in that context when he meas-
ures it against the million and odd crimes committed annually.
The war against crime is waged nationally with little prospect of
ultimate victory. A police section fights on a limited front and is
capable of winning local skirmishes. Most policemen want to do
something effective, that is why they joined. No sane person
picks the police if he wants an easy job. The police service is a
loosely-knit body with general aims. You and your section are
more closely-knit, the aims may be the same and they can be
related to a specific area. Your aims can be identified, the reduction of thefts from motor vehicles, the reduction of accidents on
a particular road. And if the group helps to set its own goals, it
is more likely to work for their attainment.

This common purpose must be attainable within the resources
available; there is little point in a sergeant and four constables in
Carlisle deciding its goal is the capture of a gang of antique thieves
in Amsterdam. It also helps to set a time scale, the reduction of
vandalism within two months, otherwise time drags on, interest
wanes, success is difficult to measure, new informal goals supplant

the formal ones. Periodic changes of goal enliven interest; one month doubling the submission of criminal intelligence, the next reducing crime on a specific beat.

So what about the rest of the job while everyone's doing his own thing? Of course the daily routine must go on, sometimes specific goals may have to be changed or even abandoned because of other commitments. Nor is it suggested that a policeman's daily work is lack-lustre. However, specific goals, extra to routine, do supply a sense of purpose all too easily lost in perpetually rising crime figures, soaring accident statistics and the frustration evoked by some of the less welcome facets of social change. Something can be done, your group can do it. Nothing lifts morale like success. The attainment of small goals can lift the spirit of a group until it is ready for anything.

Leadership affects morale in other ways. The attitudes of one member of a group affects the rest. Favouritism, harsh discipline, attacks on the dignity of one are seem as attacks on the rest if it transgresses their standards. Men develop a team spirit, thinking of "us" instead of "me" when they are certain that "us" are going to be treated the same, that a good piece of work reflects on "us", not just the one who feels the collar, that "us" are supported by the leader and regonised outside "our" circle. Thus it gives members status. Confidence develops that can overcome minor setbacks and stay the course until the goals are attained. Ideas will be thrown up that are the ingredients of many people's opinions, for after all, they probably have more collective experience than the leader. Enthusiasm will be generated, trust established which will not see a threat in every change, role conflict reduced where formal and informal goals coincide.

It is the initiative and spirit which should be praised, results should follow naturally. Care may be needed, the relationship between effort and results is far from exact. Some of the most difficult protracted enquiries end without an arrest. Some of the best arrests arise through what can only be described as sheer unadulterated luck. Too much emphasis on results in the shape of arrests and prosecutions can lower morale, encourage people to take chances, be downright self-seeking. It is for the leader to control.

Half the bother about morale comes from the nature of the policeman's work. The standard of the service to the public is as important as the results. Good morale lets a section shrug off the vagaries of a seemingly unappreciative public. It also makes any group easier to lead. If the section accepts the formal goals and values, it will enforce them, and the pressure it can exert on its members is far more powerful than anything stars and stripes can weild. The disapproval of mates cannot be shrugged off like a few choice words from the sergeant. That is why sending to Coventry is so hurtful, it deprives of status, it cuts the offender off from his fellow men, it is a public display of disapproval. There will be no uniting against the boss, for once, he is-not involved. Participation and acceptance are conditions of membership the not-so-eager have to keep up, letting down the group may become a major sin.

Any leader who has done his best and still can't get them to fall in and follow him, should consider if they are already marching in a different direction with someone else calling the tune. If they are not turned about they may get out of earshot.

5 Communication

OVER AND OUT

The intrepid Victorians travelled the world secure in their simple faith that the English language, if spoken loudly and clearly, was universally understood. The belief is still alive on the Costa Brava and all points east where the tourist trade flourishes. Nor are these the only places where it obstinately refuses to die, it is still cherished in the bastions of management. Despite all that has been said and written about communication in management, the daily failure in effective communication between managers and managed remains a major obstacle. From which, the cynics may conclude that much of what has been written and said on the subject is itself a notable failure.

Ther is no miraculous cure for the ills of communication; some of the symptoms may be recognised, the ailment does respond to sustained treatment. Because communication is between human beings, it is concerned as much with human relations as the mechanics of speaking and writing. And the first question is always what objective does a specific communication seek to achieve? The answer is always "To be understood."

Because we spend our lives speaking, and by and large getting along, because we were taught to write at school well enough for everyday use, it is tempting to think we communicate adequately. Therein lies the danger. The perfect transplant of ideas from one mind to another is perhaps the most difficult thing human beings are called on to do regularly. Nor are words the only way of conveying ideas, as anyone who has received a "how — about — it" look from the blonde at the bar can witness. Gestures and looks are misinterpreted as easily as words, as those who responded to the blonde and received something different from what they were expecting can also witness.

Before looking at communication within an organisation, consider the difficulties in making ourselves understood, a problem not confined to management by any means. To say it is ridiculous that such a simple matter should cause so much bother overlooks the fact that human beings are individuals. Who can claim that he has never had difficulties in making his wife understand his point of view? Who can say he has never had any problems persuading a child that spinach is a more beneficial food that ice cream? And if you've never had problems with promotion boards, why are you not the Chief Constable?

The difficulties arise because of the different attitudes, prejedices, beliefs and points of view on almost everything. People see things from different angles, they disagree not only on the rights and wrongs, but on all the variations in between. Human perception of any situation is formed from the way individuals have developed, their childhood, family, education, the jobs they've done, the people they've met, the experiences that have befallen them. This moulding makes individuals precisely that, a fact that cannot be ignored however much you wish it otherwise. Some people see policemen as the guardians of law and order, others as obstacles to a life of crime, others as reactionary elements holding back the advancement of society; the same figure in blue means different things to different people — and he does not have to say a word.

Human beings often think in archtypes: all Irishmen fight, all policemen are lazy, all schoolboy like sweets. It is not true of course, and if asked everyone agrees it is not. That does not stop them reacting as if all policemen are lazy, and having reacted that way they will treat policemen that way. There are energetic coppers just as there are pacifist Irishmen, yet it's difficult to communicate with a pacifist if you have classified him as pugilist and treat him as such. However individuals are classified, by race, occupation or the colour of their hair, they remain individuals to themselves, and communication is between individuals.

This is why appeals to reason usually fall on deaf ears, people are governed as much by emotion as logic, as you know when the Saturday night revels turn sour. To emotionally charged people, their view is reasonable, their attitude is logical even though it does not conform to the rules laid down by those Greek chaps a long time ago. Policemen understand this fact about human nature when dealing with the public; they sometimes overlook it when dealing with themselves.

The differences of opinion which makes Jack different from John are the foundations on which the barriers to communication are built. The list of barriers is endless, all that any manager can do is be aware of them, and not cause people to build any more.

The greatest barrier of all is the inability or unwillingness to communicate. No manager can function without effective communication. Inability can be cured; unwillingness can be treated only by self-therapy. Any manager sets the style of communication: he has to be receptive, listen to people, be aware of attitudes, watch job performance, hear what is said and sense what is implied. Willingness and ability to communicate will reduce many of the manager's barriers. The ones erected by other people cause as many difficulties.

Communication in management is usually the means of getting a job done in the way the manager requires. As well as inducing action, it may indicate a change of attitude or consideration of a point of view. There is supposedly in many people an inherent laziness, a resistance to change which has been called a fear of the unknown. Fear is a barrier which everyone erects: fear of being wrong, fear of criticism, fear of physical harm, fear of looking foolish, fear of being found wanting. The naked ape is a complicated beast, when the fear button throbs in his brain, he can genuinely misunderstand and interpret messages in a way which reduces the insistent throb to an asprin-treatable pulse. The fear can be avoided by making the unknown understandable.

Attacks on dignity, even unintentional ones, are another major barrier. A person's dignity is affronted when people won't listen to him, when he's not treated with respect, however lowly his place in the hierarchy. The child's tag "sticks and stones may hurt my bones, calling doesn't hurt me", is not true. Words wound deeply, and wounded people are not well disposed to the person who injured them. Think of the person you dislike most; would you believe something they said as readily as something from your closest friend? The attitude of the recipient towards the sender affects the way the messages are understood. Everyone builds barriers to protect their dignity, battering rams usually fail to demolish them.

One difficulty is that the barriers are not the same for each individual. Some, like the wrong word, the wrong place, the wrong time, the unintended look, even uncreased trousers, may seem beneath your attention, for you are dealing with grown men. Don't be deceived, as any comedian knows, it's not what you say, it's the way you say it that really counts. And there is one huge barrier, those crowns, pips or stripes; the quaint idea that communication not punctuated with "Sir" is insubordinate. When you are wearing badges of rank it's easy to pretend or forget they are there, others can't. A good manager keeps them in mind even though he never shows it, rank and status surround him, it is up to him to show people the way through these barriers.

For those outraged, do not despair, the police organisation is no different from the average commercial organisation where managers spend time erecting barriers of rank and status, usually they're people who could not manage without them. To some people they are important, particularly if they find it difficult to get along with other people anyway. Perhaps they have not realised the fundamental truth about communication: it is neither one way street or two track road, it is an eight lane motorway with all sorts of vehicles travelling in both directions at different speeds. Those who believe that communication is simply "telling 'em" will never be heard accurately, and they also shut out a wealth of information which could make their own job easier. Communication is sharing ideas not unloading information; it is participation in understanding. To communicate, any manager has to be receptive, and if you've let it be known that you can be approachable and no one comes, don't give up. Take another look, somewhere there's a barrier, and it may be one you've erected unintentionally, like not inviting people to sit down. You communicate as much by what you do as what you say.

Those sensing that throwing the organisation out of the window is advocated, or a one-to-one manager to managed ratio with plenty of probing to get rid of all the nasty misconceptions is necesssary, have faith. The organisational structure must be the foundation on which efficiency is based, management is the interplay of people within an organisation. It does not follow they should get so engaged in the structure that they strangle themselves.

The formal structure provides the formal communication net work. The usual family tree diagram illustrates the manager is responsible for those below him, is responsible to those above him and has to work with those level with him. The formal lines of communication are UP, DOWN and ACROSS. From the family tree, every manager should be able to determine the position of everyone else in the hierarchy and appreciate his own relative position, where his lines of communication must go. The lower down the tree, the nearer is the manager to putting his feet on the ground, more instructions are given, more specific facts received. The higher up the tree, the nearer the sky, there is more concern with policy, with trends rather than isolated events.

The leaves at the top must be sustained by the roots, inform-ation must ascend and descend, to be filtered at different levels. Sitting on some of the branches are information jackdaws who, confusing information with power, seize it to gloat in the privacy of their nests. If that's what turns them on, well, but often that information is vital to others lower down the tree, and that causes as much inefficiency as when they seize what sould be passed up for others to act upon. Running about on some branches are information magpies, gathering information to store until its needed. Like all magpies, they can never remember where they've stored it, so the tree starves. Hopping around here and there are information robins, pugnacious little things jealously guarding their own piece of branch. The only sound they ever utter is a warning to keep off, and they chase anyone who does not heed them, even those who merely want to progress from branch to branch with the news the woodman's axe is about to fall. Usually near the top of the tree is a glossy crow, too proud to hop from branch to branch, he flies straight to the one he wants. Those birds on the branches he passes never get to know what he says, even though they are responsible for those he talks to directly. Some-where there's an owl, he knows what's going on. Pretending to be asleep with his head under his wing, he hears all and sees all. He does not say anything to the other birds, he's too proud to offer advice, he rather resents being in that particular tree anyway.

There's other squawks and cheeps that all birds in the tree should understand, whatever their plumage; those sounds rarely get from the leaves to the roots without being changed. Anyone interested in organisational ornithology can think of other breeds of bird found in most trees, and the sounds they make.

And if now you're preening your feathers because you have not been classified, ask you immediate boss and your immediate subordinates. They'll tell you straight away the colour of the egg from which you hatched.

Despite imperfections, the tree's filtering process is important. No one in any organisation can know everything that's going on, in an efficient outfit no one needs to. What they do need is all the information that affects them, which is a lot more than what to do and how to do it; there's background information, shifts in policy, changes in the manager's mind which affect their work. And in communicating these, managers are communicating some-thing else important, their own attitude to communication. Like most two-way human systems, if you show you're aware of other people's needs, they'll show they're aware of yours. One word of caution: you've been in their boots before you reached your exalted rank, they've never been in yours; you should know what they want, they can only guess what you need. So if at first some of what is offered proves useless or unsuitable, don't slam the door on it. Experienced coppers know before that all important statement is taken, there's talk about all sorts of things, to remove misunderstanding, establish a basis of trust, show an attitude conducive to communication. Putting a notice up "Open for communication" means little, it has to be shown you mean business, and as any salesman knows, the best contracts are not signed on the first visit.

Every organisation also has an informal communication system, just as important as its officially recognised brother. It exists whether managers acknowledge it or not, and it will not go away because they close their eyes. It is not to be confused with "trade union" activities nor does it necessarily mean trouble; the managers who get trouble from it are usually those who deserve it. The informal structure has many factors which help managers in matters of morale, efficiency and job satisfaction. It is a phenomenon springing from the normal human desire to discuss matters of common interest. If there is no informal communication, there is no interest, and if there is no interest it is a pretty sick organisation.

With informal communication there is none of the noting and submitting then passing here and there, so it works much faster. It has other advantages: it works on face-to-face contact; it does not attempt to cope with floods of information; it seeks out from those in the know; it does not have to answer to any authority; and because it operates only by common consent, its successes are publicised and its failures forgotten. Of course, by relying on people for transmission it is prone to the same defects of misrepresentation as its formal brother, though the barriers are always lower.

The grapevine, as the system is called, is not the prerogative of the lowly. Whatever may be the ethics of feeding or tapping it, many things of interest will be found nowhere else, complaints and grievances, for instance, the key to the health of any organisation. Some managers believe sincerely that accurate feedback is impossible without listening to the grapevine; few effective managers deliberately cut themselves off from any source of information. If it is going to be used, it is best to have some idea how it works.

It is assumed that the grapevine is like the party game where a person whispers a sentence to the next in line, and everyone laughs at the final distorted corruption. This is only partially true. Unlike the party game, the essential which makes a person pass information is that HE must be interested in the contents, either because of the effect on him, or to gain admiration as a man in the know. If that essential is missing, it is unlikely the information will be passed at all. So, if four men on a section have information which affects only one, only he will pass it on. If secret information is received that the number of inspectors in a station is to be increased, everyone will pass it on because everyone in that section will be affected. Should that information be that someone, somewhere will be promoted to another station, only those qualified for promotion will show real interest. Research has shown that information carried on the average industrial grapevine was 80% accurate, though the 12% which was inaccurate contained the most important facts. The accuracy was reduced considerably when the information was emotive — something to kept in mind with formal communication as well. Many communication problems arise simply because a manager has failed to recognise that information, or the lack of it, can arouse passionate emotions. More than one strike has been threatened because of alteration to tea breaks. Because the grapevine deals directly with people who know, it can crack the tightest managerial security screen, and has an all-embracing capacity.

What the grapevine actually transmits can be useful or harmful to a manager. If he's going to feed it, obviously it must be through someone interested enough to pass the message on; if he's going to tap it, he should be aware of the emotional overtones. To be caught misusing it, or to over-trust it, are among the cardinal sins of all managers.

Part of the mistrust of the grapevine is based on one of its undesirable features — rumour. Sometimes it seems that this is the only feature, though there is a distinction.

The grapevine passes information which, despite inaccuracies, is based on fact. Rumour has no real basis of fact, it needs not only interest, but uncertainty or ambiguity. It follows the more any organisation tells the people in it, the less uncertainty and ambiguity, hence less rumour. Not that all employees can know everything that's going on, they don't expect to, they realise some things must be kept quiet. The reason informal communication, rumour or not, becomes distorted is that each recipient picks out what he thinks are the salient points. In doing that, he treats it exactly like formal communication. To attract the attention of others, the information is embellished, the emphasis changed, perhaps credited to persons more likely to give it credence. The next person repeats the process. It is easy to see how minor affairs swell to mammoth proportions, and the less the basis of fact, the easier it grows, for as the newspaper men say, facts are sacred, they can't be distorted as easily as pure invention. At this stage, a manager's denial of the rumour is often taken as confirmation of its truth by subordinates, whereas a few facts would kill it stone dead. Truth and facts are never bedfellows of uncertainty and ambiguity.

Rumour can be a problem, it is the touchstone of the malcontent in any organisation. Rumour is like a boil on the neck, everyone has one some time or other, yet it rarely lasts long on a healthy body. In treating it, resist the temptation to cut out vital organs which may be needed later.

At this stage, you may be wondering how anyone communicates, with all the difficulties mentioned. Yet, the job gets done, and very well done on occasions. True, though until it gets done well on every occasion, there's need for care with communication. It is the biggest stumbling block for every manager, and you don't want to be one who does a good job occasionally.

Let's turn to the three methods of communication.

1. VISUAL The Chinese have a saying that one picture is worth a thousand words. One diagram, one graph, or one plan can save hundreds of tedious explanations, re-readings and misunderstanding. It is a form of communication too little used in the lower echelons of management. It does not have to be in glorious technicolour, although colour helps. A simple graph can arouse interest in dull statistics, a rough sketch can bring a traffic problem to life, a diagram explain at a glance how equipment can be improved. People look at easy-to-understand information who would never read half a page of the most concise report. You can see this in the notices which adorn every police station, a good example of visual communication, though sadly, often how not to do it. Nobody looks at the notice board which has nothing worthwhile to say, where anyone sticks up anything, often on top of the yellow curling notice about last year's pay rise.

Visual display is a specialised field, no one is suggesting you enrol for night classes or stagger home from the library with an armful of books. You can learn a great deal from looking critically at the visual displays around you, on the bus, the hoardings, the newspapers, in your police station, and deciding for yourself which is effective and why. Then, you'll have to practice.

The second aspect of visual communication is summed up in the phrase "actions speak louder than words." As a manager you will communicate enthusiasm, energy, understanding and a sense of purpose. Words, however charming, do not convince people for long; men are what they do, not what they say. Managers communicate every time they do, or don't do, something. No one likes working under a microscope, the temptation to say one thing and do another dangles in front of every manager, sometimes it may even be necessary. If your subordinates mutter they can't hear what you're saying for the noise of what you're doing, one means of communication is cancelling out another, and they'll be entitled to put whatever interpretation they like. Hard luck perhaps, but managers are on a pedestal; bad communication is the surest way to make it crumble beneath feet of clay.

2. WRITTEN. Paperwork is an emotive word, everyone complains there's too much, yet it grows like some malignant monster. It is the formal structure which generates this life blood of the organisation, all any manager can do is ensure he dosen't add to the burden so the life blood becomes a clot. Statutory requirements, necessary policies, dictate some of the endless records and reports which each section collects. But not all of them, not every report submitted is necessary, though once it gets into the system it takes up someone's time and effort. Somone may be you. The truth is that the greater the mass of paper floating about, the less of it is read. People boggle at the size of the in tray, take a deep breath — and go and do something else.

Don't throw away that new ball point with the seven different colours just yet, managers do involve themselves in the art of written communication, you will not be the exception. Many managers involve themselves too lightly, they do not write what they mean, or do not mean what they write, then complain they are misunderstood. There are simple rules which help in the planning of written communication which do not depend on an expensive education or a wide vocabulary. Your words are you, it is your communication. Ask yourself:

a) Why am I communicating at all? To report facts, to make a record, to ask for instructions, to give orders, because I want someone else to do something. Each report has a purpose, getting that purpose clear in your mind is a first step. You may find at this stage the report is unnecessary.

b) *Who is the recipient?* Not always the person you address it to, this should be the person who will take action on it however it is addressed, the Research & Planning chap at H.Q., the Chief Superintendant, the cadet who collects for the childrens' party.

c) *What does he know about it?* To answer this question, imagine you are sitting in his chair, and your report is on the desk. You do not need to quote the Theft Act to a Chief Inspector, you may have to quote a word or a section if you're arguing why the mayor's son should be prosecuted. Everyone in the organisation has background knowledge, you're wasting their time and yours, thereby raising a barrier, if you tell them too much of what they already know.

d) *What do I need to tell him?* Still sitting in the reader's chair, what does he need to know so he can carry out the purpose of the communication. This should follow naturally from the previous answers. It's a fine judgment, leaving out essentials, creates as big a barrier as overloading with irrelevancies.

e) *What is the conclusion?* This should follow naturally as well. As a manager, you should be capable of coming to a conclusion, a recommendation, suggestion or instruction. Your reader will not always agree, but that's better than leading him to an ending which is missing. You can not complain you don't get what you want if you don't say what it is. It's surprising how many written communications shy away at the last fence from committing the writer to something definite.

These questions should be asked before the dictaphone is switched on or your calloused thumb hits the first key of the typewriter. Many people write before they've thought what they want to say, as if it was so easy that no thought was involved. That's often the impression left in the reader's mind.

When the instructions, report or whatever is complete, read it through to check it against the questions as well as for typing errors. Have you expressed yourself clearly? Could it be misunderstood? Is it concise? The shorter the communication, the easier to understand. Of all tools, words are the most ill-used; some of the best ideas have been fashioned so crudely they were unrecognisable.

There are many books on effective use of words, this isn't one of them. You'll have to turn to them to notice how to avoid the fog and pomposity which overcomes some people when they pick up a pen, "how to use the right word in the right place and how to string them together" how to pursue a logical course from beginning to end. It may help to mention there's a school of thought which believes those managers who can express themselves progress the furthest. As you can't be constantly hobnobbing with the great, dropping little gems of wit at appropriate moments, your best chance of success is in written communication. And perfection is acquired through practice.

Part of every manager's written communication is comment on other people's reports, what the army calls "staff work". Apart from checking that the job was done properly, that all the i's are dotted, staff work is summarising the issues so that a decision can be made without ploughing through reams of paper. The higher up the tree, the more paper to read, the more decisions to be made for other people. Don't shed tears for those who shoulder this load, though you will earn their gratitude and the reputation of a good manager by reducing it. It will also be good practice, you're not going to stay in your present rank for ever. Staff work is something police managers do not excel in, partly because they're not expected to do it. Be proud, you can sum up the arguments, you can suggest a course of action, you can point out the likely consequences.

Some of the stuff which drops on your desk is incapable of staff work, the wrong form, facts missed out, too many irrelevant details. You've seen it many times. Considering the amount of paper you complain of, some of it is despoiled wantonly. By all means send it back for correction, but communicate why, say what you require. In communicating to those for whom you are responsible how to communicate effectively, you are lightening your load, investing for the future, and improving the flow of blood along the arteries of the organisation.

3. SPOKEN. At the grass roots of management, the bulk of communication is face-to-face, often with little time to formulate the message. There are those who think without speaking, and there are the other sort. Neither communicate effectively. There is always time for a moment to think what communication is needed on this occasion.

The same question should be asked before you speak as before you write, it sometimes helps to plan what you're going to say. With spoken communication you can see the other people in the process, gauge their reaction, re-phrase, emphasise, even change what you are saying as you go along; most important of all, you can ensure you have been understood. It is worth repeating that the choice of words, intonation, gestures ana facial expressions are part of verbal communication. This accompaniment can be used to reinforce what you're saying, or detract from it; sometimes people like the words but don't care for the time. Flat words on paper will bear many interpretations, people read not only between the lines, they read between the lines that are not there. The accompaniment is important. Try saying "come in and sit down" in as many tones as possible. You can make it sound anything from autocratic to pornographic. This all points that you should try to understand your audience, be it one man or a hundred, try to forsee barriers that may be there and avoid building any more, avoid imperious do's and don'ts, talk with them not at them address them by name. No one likes to be talked down to, credited, even by implication, with less intelligence skill or humanity than they possess, treated as if they had no dignity, or not important. To themselves, they are the most important person in the world, and if you are a good manager, they are vital to you. You do not insult intelligence when you make it simple to understand, the greatest masters of the language are precisely that because they conceal their greatness in simplicity of language.

To do all this of course, you have to give others a chance to open their mouths. The best talkers are also the best listeners, anyone thinking too much of what he wants to say does not hear what is said to him. There is a difference between listening and hearing, as anyone plagued by transistor radios knows. Listening helps to sense and demolish barriers, yours and theirs; people under no obligation to speak only do so when they know someone will listen to what they say. Spoken communication is flexible, quick and cheap, perhaps too cheap, for like many things in the Land of Plenty, quantity is confused with quality. At the lower levels of management, it is perhaps the most effective means of communication, through it you get to know your men, you learn what is going on, the facts, the background, why things go wrong, what you can do about them. They are the ones actually doing the job, they know as much about it as anyone, their opinion is valid, insight and understanding are not a divine right of managers.

The majority of the orders and instructions you give will be verbal. You will already have guessed that telling someone to do something is not enough. People do genuinely misunderstand. The more information you give about why, how, where, when, the better they will understand. You must not insult them, but you can check they really have understood without having them repeat it word for word like a nursery class. And you can keep checking, as with all communication, that you have been effective. It is a continuous process, not a "now hear this" and switch off.

One of the most important jobs any manger has is the interpreter of information from Higher up the tree. It may be that Headquarters insist in writing as if the giveaway in the cornflakes was a dictionary, the job has still to be done so it may as well be done with a will. Your subordinates have not your expertise in deciphering the tablets from the mountain, and to them, its your interpretation which counts. Tact and patience are required in sorting out the 99 sections and deciding which apply to you and which don't. If it is that long, feed it in digestible pieces, people choke on too much at one time. Tact and patience are required to put over something which you know they won't agree with; if you've built up a basis of trust, are aware of the pitfalls and establish an attitude conducive to communication, you'll get by. Pinning it on a crowded notice board for them to read is neither interpretation nor communication.

Understanding what you want to communicate, why it's necessary, points out the method. Sometimes it will be all three, giving them written and visual material to study before it is discussed for instance. If you must reach a large number of people, or make a record for future reference it must be written; it is thought by many that written communication carries greater authority (anything in black and white must be true). If it is necessary to prove the authority to others, for example by a signature, then writing is necessary. With skill written communication can be made precise, it can be drafted, edited and revised. If the personal touch is wanted, or flexibility and simplicity, if the relationship between people is such that there is much personal contact, spoken communication will be better. If you want an interchange of ideas and opinion, they become tedious in writing, most people believe they can make themselves better understood by speaking, there is still something about committing it to paper which has overtones of doom. If you want informality, you will rarely achieve it on paper; if you use the grapevine, you can't use paper.

Laying the basis for communication is using the correct medium, for as they say, the medium is the message. Only the manager can decide which is right for that occasion. It is easy, and sometimes cowardly, to hide behind a piece of paper when face-to-face contact is required or expected. A look or word at the time may be more effective than a memo six days later; or that memo may be the exact means of communication. The responsibility for establishing effective communication rests squarely on the manager, it is not an easy one; if you succeed, most of the rest of management will fall into place.

6 *Decision Making*

Don't Ask Me

Life is full of decisions, what time to get up in the morning, what to have for breakfast, how many spoonfuls of sugar in the coffee. Such decisions are often taken without thought, and the consequences, even if the decision is wrong, are relatively unimportant. To a diabetic, a few too many grains of sugar can have dire results, whether thay be carefully weighed or not. If it is the diabetic who has over sweetened himself, sympathy may be offered, though sooner or later, someone will say it was his own fault.

Manager's decisions are similar, they, too, can have dire consequences for the organisation, whether weighed carefully or made with no thought at all. There is one important difference — managers' decisions affect other people. Think back through your last working day, how many decisions did you make? It is a surprising number. And how many did you think about, examining all the possibilities? Only a fraction of the total, if you scored at all. Of course there are decisions where there can be only one answer, but they are much rarer than they appear, particularly if required from someone who won't commit himself, or does not recognise a problem when he sees it.

All managers make some decisions on what they would call "instinct". The decision may appear to come off the cuff but is more likely to be based on past experience and recognition of the background to the problem from which the nature of the problem itself and the remedial action required can be deduced. This apparently automatic reaction must be based on sound background knowledge with an ability to marshal the key factors of the situation mentally. It is usually limited to minor day-to-day problems. If used as the normal process of decision making it has obvious dangers. The man who believes he can manage entirely by instinct is not normally a thinking man, or he would not hold that belief at all.

No one likes working for bosses who are indecisive, it makes them insecure, apprehensive about both present and future. It makes them frustrated when they are held up waiting for someone else to make up his mind. It causes resentment when they have to make decisions which they feel should have been made for them, even more so if they are then criticised for it. Some of the decisions will be made by the informal leaders, not necessarily to enhance the progress of the organisation, and may then cause even more problems to wait in the queue for decisions. Indecision saps morale as effectively as a string of bad decisions. Confidence in the leadership is under-mined, particularly when events at last force the hurried ill conceived decision people feel they had the right to expect a month or so before in more sober times. Indecision affecting individuals, their hopes and fears, is a major de-motivating factor, giving the impression that no one cares.

And if you are one of those waiting for the new generation of computers, they do not make decisions, they only provide fast accurate information from which managers make decisions.

It goes without saying, no one is right all the time, if there are right and wrong decisions. There are valid and invalid decisions, there are workable and unworkable decisions, but a right decision is difficult to define. However, to save needless repetition, the word right will be used. The frequency of right decisions can be improved by understanding something of the decision making process. This is concerned with action, not head-scratching, although that may be part of the process. Announcing to a credulous section that a new decision has been conceived achieves nothing unless it can be implemented, and it won't be unless it is born fully formed and recognisable. Naturally, people find it easier to implement decisions they agree with, and even easier those they helped to make.

In operational situations, problems may demand instant answers, any action is better than none. These are comparatively rare, there's been more than one occasion when all the available man-power has gone charging off to the burglary, leaving no one to man the roadblock through which the culprits must drive. Fire brigade policing causes more problems than it solves. Yes, sometimes it is necessary, more often it's justified because no one took the time or trouble to work out a better solution. Too much instinct decision making?

In a sense, management problems are more difficult. On the face of them, they appear to be concerned with one thing, but this is just a symptom, and if only that is treated, the spots will appear somewhere else, perhaps a different colour, perhaps a different size, but the same spots. In one section, the responsibility for submitting the reports was changed to the station sergeant, although the patrol sergeant retained the responsibility of supervising the beat work. Things began to go wrong, the station sergeant complained about the way incidents were dealt with, the patrol sergeant retorted that it was a simple over-exercise of authority the station sergeant didn't have. The row simmered, boiling over now and then. The chief inspector let it go on, hoping they would sort it out themselves, finally deciding that it was a clash of personalities which could be solved by moving one of them to another shift. Soon after, it happened again, with different sergeants, and convinced there was a malignant pettiness virus at large, the chief inspector moved these sergeants to different shifts. Was the problem one of personalities, or one of organisation? Reporting incidents is one way of exercising control over the way they are dealt with, which everyone agreed was the patrol sergeants job, so why give his control system to someone else, for everyone also agreed that the patrol sergeant could not attend each incident personally. The system was changed, the spots disappeared from the sergeants' faces, although they suspected they'd suffered needlessly from a wrong diagnosis. Another section seemed quite incapable of getting reports to Headquarters on time. The system of submission and collation was reviewed, the organisation tinkered with, none of which seemed to have any effect. Everyone was convinced it must be the system, so more amendments, more changes of plan, and still nothing improved. Then it was discovered that the girl clerk had to rush for her bus each evening, she'd no time to struggle with large envelopes in small letter boxes, so she did not post them until the following morning, or left them at home for her mother to post. To the clerk, they were just letters. Allowing her to leave five minutes earlier each evening solved all the problems which organisational change could not.

You will also have seen ideals confused with ideas, and the rashness with which it is tried to implement them. Ideas are not decisions. Ideas are ten a penny, decisions are much more expensive. An inspector passed a casual remark about a better system of charging personal radio batteries. It was four in the morning, one or two more joined in the conversation, an idea was born. With all the enthusiasm of a first time-father, the inspector's final comment was adulatory about his new offspring. Some took this as an instruction to try it, others thought it had been just hurrying the clock to finishing time, some didn't understand the point he'd been making. Some tried to make the idea work, some didn't, some half-tried, some thought their own idea much better. You know the rest, batteries were damaged through overcharging or stayed flat. In three weeks the operational efficiency was in jeopardy, a far worse problem than the original one. The idea was implemented later with complete success, once the right question had been asked and the right answer found.

It had been said that the camel is a horse designed by a committee. Beware of so-called committee decisions, they are a favourite source of problem-creating ideas. The difficulties of setting up large committees based on a consensus of opinion this to gain that principle to reach practical decisions are well known. So the committee which designed the camel did not do a bad job, for a committee. The point is a simple one: where there's a hint of committee about a rash of spots, be suspicious.

From this you will have deduced that the first step in decision-making is not answering the questions you were posed, but asking if you were posed the right questions. The right answers to the wrong questions are just as unhelpful as the wrong answers to the right questions. Anyone can see spots, finding what causes them is a job for a good manager. If you think of all the ailments from which any organisation can suffer, you will realise that their manifestations are endless. But you know your organisation, you are sensitive to the structure and the people within it, you know where problems can be expected.

Having isolated the cause of the spots, look carefully at it. There is a temptation to overlook the obvious, the daily routine, the things you've always done. Don't take them for granted, they may have been fine, fifty years or fifty days ago, it doesn't follow they must be now. Especially be careful if the cause is your own previous decision, there is a tendency to look at our own creations with distorted vision, don't put a halo round them. They could have been just right for the problem they treated, but are they right for the current one? A good description of the autocrat is the man who only had one idea in his life, and good or bad, applied it to everything.

Test the problem by forecasting what would happen if nothing was done about the cause. The answer is probably the key factor. If the cause can be traced back in time, try and discover the change from the previous practice which now presents problems. Again, the answer is likely to be the key factor. If the Chief Inspector had used these tests with personality-clashing sergeants, he may have saved everyone's temper.

The key factor is the central piece in the jigsaw into which all the other pieces interlock. Leave the central piece where it is, the others may be changed, though they'll never really fit. Change the central piece and every other piece can be changed. Determining the key factor is essential.

Before attempting a decision, information is needed. It is surprising how many policemen, who rightly refuse to jump to conclusions in detecting crime until they have painstakingly assembled the facts, will leap straight to management decisions without facts at all. "There must be more thefts from vehicles this year, we had six last week" is no more a fact than "it must be him, he was nearest" is proof of murder. There are fifty two weeks in a year, human memory rarely carries a weekly breakdown with precision. Of course, assembling facts can be a laborious business, there's always a temptation to omit some, or use them incomplete. All police forces keep statistics, facts and records on a wide variety of matters. They are usually available if you explain why you need them. One computer print out may save weeks of reading through musty station records, although if they are the only way, it has to be done. And facts include what people think about situations, their attitudes, their capabilities.

Without apologising for what has been said, it is acknowledged that time is sometimes of the very essence of the decision to be made. You have to make do with those facts which can be gathered in that time. Maybe the time limit is imposed on you, maybe the problem is so serious that you have to act. Only you can decide, it is no time to be poring over the design drawings when the ship is slipping under the waves.

If the facts are not available, because you have not time, or they do not exist, you will have to guess intelligently. If you know how your organisation works it is not as hazardous as it seems, although the risks are obvious. Not all equations have enough information to give you the value of "x", however good your maths. The risk is reduced if you work from the known to the unkown instead of picking with a pin. With knowledge, intelligent guesswork can be an able substitute for facts. It is essential to recognise which are facts and which are guesses, so if the final decision is not as good as it ought to be, you will know where to start checking.

However, the facts themselves may tell you little. They have to be interpreted. Are thefts from vehicles increasing or decreasing, is there any pattern to area, time of day, type of vehicle, type of property? Do any of these patterns relate to any other? Do the complaints about delayed arrival at incidents relate to everyone, or certain individuals, are they of one age or experience group, are the vehicles the same, is the radio operator who sends them the same? It is the interpretation, the arranging, the classifying which is important, not least because it gets rid of those facts which are irrelevant Provided that time is not a critical factor, as when the ship is sinking, that spent on assembling the facts is never wasted. Many decisions would have been better if their authors had spent more on research and less on developemnt. A hasty decision may appear to save time, it may waste endless hours for other people, and soon it will be back on your desk, waiting to be done again. Short cuts are not always the best route.

From your identification of the key factor and your interpretation of the information you have gathered, you can work out a series of solutions. Don't at this stage be constrained, let your imagination wander, take nothing for granted, particularly the obvious. Imagination is not just concerned with make believe, the ordinary can be exciting from another angle, some of the greatest revelations have been there for all to see, waiting for the imaginative eye to look. Alternative solutions will suggest themselves, however unrealistic they may seem, put them down. There are a wide range of alternatives to most questions in life, very little is black or white to the exclusion of the colours of the rainbow in between. Reason out the alternatives; if A, then B, if the proposed pedestrian crossing is placed outside the butchers shop, the bus stop will have to be moved; moving the bus stop in a northerly direction will mean greater congestion; moving it in a southerly direction will be to a narrower part of the street, therefore the pedestrian crossing placed outside the butcher's shop will cause other problems. And do not overlook the decision not to do anything. A decision not to make a decision is itself a decision, something entirely different from not taking action because of lack of courage or ability. When all the reasoning has been completed, it may well be that the decision to take no action is the right one.

Beware of the only alternative, the solution which blocks all others. It may be right, it is probably an appeal to emotions, a preconceived idea seeking respectability, an easy way out trying to gain confidence.

Some of your alternatives will be factual, all will depend not only on the accuracy of your information and the intelligence of your guesses, but also on the length of time the information will stay accurate, and intelligent. Perhaps the eventual decision will lay down policy or systems for many years, perhaps it will solve an isolated problem of the moment. The final decision should be accurate, long term or short term, the process is the same.

Having assembled the alternatives, now is the time to examine the constraints upon them. Some may offend Standing Orders or other rules of the organisation. Some may require resources neither available nor obtainable. One constraint often overlooked by policemen is cost, there is a price on policemen's time, the salary of that extra typist, the more frequent servicing of vehicles. Then if you've gathered your information properly, you'll know the cost. Your authority is another constraint, for instance, you may decide the best solution is to change some long-established practice of the C.I.D., but if you've no authority over them you are faced with a choice of passing up the decision to the level where it can be implemented, or seeking a decision which you can implement yourself. Passing the decision up should always be done if you're convinced it is the right one, albeit there is no guarantee that it will be implemented as you would wish, or that the person implementing it will be as careful about his decisions as you have been. It is a sad, yet well-known fact that in many organisations minor decisions are taken at too high a level, the Chief Inspector giving the cadet an hour off, the Assistant Chief Constable personally authorising the purchase of a packet of screws. You know your organisation, in this situation it is your authority not your ability which counts, even though the spots are brightest on your face. There's many a man however, prospered by presenting the problem with right decision attached, particularly if he wasn't too eager for public applause. There are more mundane constraints, your boss's bloody-mindedness for instance. You should know how he thinks, if you hit him on the one nerve that makes him jump, is that the best solution? If he's a stickler for time — keeping, it will affect the decisions you take on time-keeping discipline. There is no point in trying to ignore his effect, nor is there much chance of you changing his attitude. Complete cures may be impossible if the patient is to live a happy life, getting rid of spots at the expense of paralysis is not recommended. The structure of the organisation is another constraint. Must police forces have a hybrid structure of police and civilian staff. Since the civilian staff provide many of the support services vital to the operational role, yet are governed by different procedures, a different discipline, a different approach to the job, it is useless to treat them as police officers. It is essential to understand how the twin structures interact, both impose constraints, neither can be overlooked, a painful process unless some degree of sympathy and expertise is used.

Although the decision will be made by you, it will be implemented by the people you manage, and their reaction can be a constraint. The police force is full of good decisions which don't work in practice because people won't implement them. There's no disobedience, nor eyeball to eyeball contact, they are not carried out the way it was intended because of lack of motivation, or prejudice, or lack of faith in them. An inspector had the reasonable belief that his equivalents in the Special Constabulary would benefit from working the beat in company with regular constables. The Special Inspectors could then better train and supervise their own men. What the inspector overlooked was that to the public, the man with the highest rank was in charge, even though that man was the first to admit that he hadn't a thimbleful of the regular's professional expertise. The constables felt their status was challenged, required nominally to go through the motions of respecting rank, they were still responsible for their own beat. Soon the beat men could always find some cast iron reason why the Special Constables should go with someone else. The scheme slipped quietly into disuse, because the constraints upon it, the attitude of those who were to implement it, had not been considered. The best solution can rarely be that which people genuinely resent. You know the people who will implement your decisions, whoever they are, you should be able to gauge their reaction if you're managing effectively.

On a broader front, operational duties are carried out in public. The work of all police forces depends on a general degree of goodwill on the part of that public, and it is no secret there are pressure groups who regard themselves as necessary watchdogs over police activities. In industry public relations are entrusted to highly-trained specialists, in the police service the way the day-to-day routine is carried out is itself public relations, without always the time to plan the right words, the right moves, the right time. Public opinion can be a severe constraint upon a public service. The consequences of ignoring it can be severe.

These constraints will mean that many of the alternatives disqualify themselves, perhaps leaving one solution. In practice, you will be left with two or three. Then you must judge which will better cure the illness of the organisation, even if it requires surgery. There is a risk in all operations, it is reduced in a healthy patient. It may require courage to operate, it may be that the right decision is going against current principles or what is "laid down in the book". You will have taken the general background of the problem into account already, the decision will have to be seen against this background, more so in short-term problems. It is only against the background that the effectiveness of your decision can be judged — and that you will judge other people's.

Having come up with your right decision, you now face the hardest part of the process, that which will tax all your managerial skill. Your decision has to be implemented by other people. They must understand it, telling them to do it is not enough. If it involves major departures from established practice, an innovation outside their previous experience they must understand the issues, what it is designed to remedy, what you expect the results to be. You will need to coach them along, be patient as they grow accustomed to the new computer form they have to fill in. In some cases, you may be better to introduce it stage by stage. Of course it's not confusing to you, you've lived with it for a long time; it may be confusing to the people who're going to make it work if you ask them to swallow too much at one bite. Their pace is the right one for them. If you hurry them too much, you'll risk them loosing interest.

As you coach along your brainchild, you'll see problems arising, perhaps through misunderstanding, perhaps you hadn't all the information you needed, perhaps your guesses weren't accurate, perhaps the situation's changed. Resist the temptation to be proud, everyone knows the midnight oil you burnt, that still doesn't make the unworkable work. Be prepared to modify, to accept a changed situation. If a little tuning won't get it running smoothly, it will be back to stage one of the process:

a) Identify the problem
b) Get the facts — or as many as time, circumstances and costs allow
c) Weigh the facts —
d) Work out the alternatives
e) Examine the constraints
f) Decide upon a course of action
g) Test it by putting it into action
h) Follow it up.

Nobody's perfect, organisational spots do not vanish if the wrong medicine's prescribed. The best doctors are those humble enough to look for something else when their cure is not working. It is no consolation that the doctor discovered it was measles and not mumps, the day after the patient died.

Decision-making is a learning tool. In this respect management is like the common law, built up from a series of decisions. As with the law, each must be constantly challenged if it is to remain valid. Every manager must be his own advocate, examining his past decisions to discover what he can learn from them to serve him in the future. Even bad decisions have experience to offer, probably being more indicative of the process than the good ones. No one is right all the time, mistakes become more bearable if they appease with lessons for the future.

Effective, accurate decisions are the most critical of the tasks you have to perform. Make them well, and you'll earn your corn, respect from subordinate and superior as well as achieving personal satisfaction. Gain a reputation for courage to make decisions, and humility to acknowledge the bad ones, and you'll be forgiven for those you prefer to forget.

Make all your decisions badly, or don't make any at all, and everyone will wonder just what it was that got you promoted.

7 Delegation

The one man band drones on

There's been so much preached about delegation it's become to the manager what sex is to the teenager, he's been brainwashed that everyone does it quite naturally. When sex is mentioned, people think of different things: when delegation is mentioned managers have different ideas. By delegation a manager may mean nothing more than giving someone a job to do; or making the same decisions and coming to the same conclusions as the manager would have done on the facts; or getting someone to do what the manager has no authority to do himself; or passing a job over lock stock and barrel, then washing his hands of it entirely.

Before defining delegation, there are two mis-conceptions about delegation in the police organisation. Incidentally, for those attracted by the mention of sex, it does not appear again. It is sometimes said that the organisational structure, the system, prevents delegation. The boundary between a constable and sergeant is too well defined, constables cannot do sergeants' jobs. What happens when the station sergeant is at all those conferences and is not replaced? Presumably the job stops or the inspector does it? Who then does the inspector's? Is there so little to do that one man can do both? (Who whispered redundancy?) Usually, an experienced constable does the sergeant's job.

The second misconception is confusion between legal and organisational responsibilities. Every Constable in law is responsible for his own actions, and as Chief Constables enjoy reminding you, in law every policeman is a constable regardless of rank. Within the organisation every sergeant and inspector is responsible to those above them for the work of their subordinates, a responsibility a thousand times wider than the legal one for individual acts and omissions. The burglar alarm goes off, Sergeant Nogood makes a mess of getting cars and men to the right place at the right time, and the real thief escapes. Nevertheless, Constable Overeager arrests the vicar. As the inspector, you are responsible for the sergeant's mismanagement, although no legal responsibility attaches to anyone for that. Constable Overeager is personally liable for the vicar's damages. Yet, as the person in charge of the operation would you have no responsibility to the organisation for Over-eager's actions? Would you have no questions for either him or Nogood? You can be certain of one thing, someone would be seeking answers from you, for you are accountable to your boss.

These misconceptions sometimes distinguish the police manager from his industrial cousin. When the police manager says the system will not allow delegation, the sad assumption follows that the organisation is not well-managed, it's firing on only two or three cylinders. Delegation will be a last resort, too little and too late, when the situation reaches panic proportions, when all the sergeants have gone to that conference. All managers, police and industrial, delegate sometimes, they could not do their job other-wise. Sometimes they guiltily deny that is what they are doing, as if they had been caught with a buxom policewoman on their knee. Sometimes they are simply unaware that they are delegating, so it is a hit-or-miss cockshy. Often, they don't delegate when they should, then blame the system or anything else they can bring to mind.

Delegation is necessary to every manager, to each organisation. It is not reserved for the boardroom or the Chief Constable's Office. If anything should attract managers to the study of delega-tions it is the promise that on occasions·it will stop them behaving like a certain fly with blue hindquarters.

Just to make sure everyone understands the same meaning, first some definitions:

Delegation   the process whereby a group or individual transfer to another group or individual the duty of carry-ing out a particular action.

Let there be no doubt in any manager's mind, delegation is entrusting some part of management to subordinates. It is the duty which is transferred, not the responsibility.

Responsibility is the task the manager is given within the organ-isation, his command, his function. It comes to him through the organisational structure.

Tasks are delegated. No one can divest himself of responsibility through delegation, that stays with the manager. The Chief Inspec-tor in charge of a sub division is responsible for the conduct and job performance of that sub division irrespective of the tasks he has delegated to the inspector or the bright young sergeant out in the sticks. What must be delegated is authority.

Authority allows managers to ask others to perform tasks. It gives managers right of access to the resources and information of the organisation.

Authority is not always worn on the sleeve, though no one can manage without it. This is obvious: if people are in a position to refuse orders or decline tasks, management is impossible.

Accountability is a person's liability for his use of authority, resources, and decisions.

Accountability exists in every organisation between people and their boss, right through the structure to the top. It does not depend upon delegation, though it becomes specific in a delegated task. It is simply the obligation to justify job performance. A subordinate is always accountable, there is no special transfer.

Well, you may think, it was quite clear before they started explaining it. Nevertheless, the problem area can be seen irrespective of definitions: a manager has to trust subordinates, he has to take the brickbats for their failure, while too much control, too much interference destroys the principle of delegation. It has been described as crawling out to the end of a branch, and giving subordinates a saw. It doesn't mean the manager has no recourse, he can make his displeasure known through the subordinate's accountability, which is what happens in practice. The manager cannot hide his responsibility, and as it remains his he cannot hide behind the subordinate. If you think that's unfair and you will have nothing to do with delegation, be patient, it is an essential part of leadership, there are valid reasons why it must operate that way. The nature of the process becomes clearer by understanding the three main reasons why subordinates fail in delegated tasks:

   a) The task has been badly communicated
   b) The subordinate has not been given sufficient authority.
   c) The subordinate has insufficient skill or knowledge.

a) Communication is the hobbyhorse of anyone who mentions management, suffice it here to point out again its vital importance. No one can be expected to do a job unless he understands what it is. Obvious? Then why is it so often overlooked? Perhaps because all managers make assumptions that people have clear pictures in their minds of what is expected. If the manager could get inside those minds, he would see an entirely different picture, sometimes, total confusion.

It is not enough to toss out the job in a few ill-chosen words, nor merely outline it. The subordinate is entitled to know where the job begins and ends, what limitations are placed upon him by the manager, what limitations are implied by the organisation, what the time scale of the job is, whether intermediate reporting is required. For instance, C.I.D. do not disclose details of informants, sending someone to ferret out such information would cut across the limitations imposed by the organisation. If it was a task involving the re-allocation of rest days, and the time is not ripe to discuss it with those likely to be affected, he should be told, as a limitation put on him by the manager.

The subordinate is entitled to know what is in the manager's mind, is it a general picture of accidents in the division or detailed statistics; how far back is he expected to go in compiling those statistics, what is the purpose of the tasks being delegated; whether the task of servicing all burglar alarms is being delegated, or there are some where the manager will personally take charge. These limitations must be stated, together with instructions where implied limitations may be encountered, for the manager should know them better than a subordinate. If you, the manager, have not made the task clear, it will be a remarkable coincidence if it is carried out as you intended. It is up to you to make sure you are both on the same wavelength.

Communication also means opening up channels through which the subordinate can report back progress or problems, through which the manager can offer advice and exercise some control. However crystal clear it may have been made at the outset, there will be little snags along the way; there's no point in spoiling a promising ship for a ha'porth of needed tar. The subordinate needs to feel that he has not been abandoned, that the manager still retains interest. Reporting back and checking progress need be little more than a few questions from time to time, provided they do not take the initiative from the subordinate who should be doing the job. It is simply a question of degree, and you are the manager, you are responsible, you must use your judgment on that.

b) Lack of authority is also overlooked. Delegation is the transfer of a duty, it becomes self-defeating if that duty cannot be performed because the necessary authority has not or cannot be transferred. Like justice, the transfer must not only be done, it must also be seen to be done by others in the organisation. Written instructions may amount to a visible transfer, although it may also be implied from the relative positions of the manager and subordinate. In acting upon the burglar alarm, Sergeant Nogood has no personal authority to direct Sergeant Doright; the authority is implied because the inspector has delegated the job of servicing burglar alarms, and Sergeant Doright knows this. Failure to pass sufficient authority publicly can have consequences other than the predestined failure of the task. It means the subordinate can be challenged when he wants access to the resources of the organisation or the co-operation of other people. If the challenges are successful, the poor subordinate begins to wonder about the standing of the fellow who has sent him on the wild goose chase; although he knows who he is acting for, those who slam the door in his face appear neither to know nor care. The subordinate may be unaware he is suffering from bad delegation, all he realises is that he can't finish the task he was given to do. Then he begins to doubt his ability, his self confidence creaks, his enthusiasm groans. Suppose you, as an inspector, need to make a detailed study of all the beats in your sub division. Up to your ears in organising the Scouts Annual Parade, you delegate the task to Sergeant Doright. He finds the Crime Prevention Sergeant is too busy or cannot be bothered to dig out the crime figures for the last two years; the clerk at Headquarters is awfully sweet, though she will not give information from the personal records because no one below the rank of inspector can have access to it; the local surveyor is doubtful about helping Doright, he has always dealt with you before and would like to again. In these circumstances, do you expect Sergeant Doright to lay the detailed study on your desk in seven days time? It is not fanciful, it happens too often for comfort. The tragedy is that Sergeant Doright wanted to do what had been delegated. First time out he came up against a brick wall. With ingenuity he got round it, to be immediately faced with another. Delegation should not be an obstacle course, they fray too many tempers, waste too much time. By some managers Old Doright would be blamed for not accomplishing his task. Next time he's given one he may show some reluctance to accept it. From there it is an easy step to assume he is lazy or lacks confidence, and that is another assumption that's not true. And, what sort of picture of the organisation has been given to those outside it when the Sergeant was sent to represent it without the authority to do so?

c) Absence of skill or knowledge was the third common reason for failure of delegation. The relationship between delegation is like that between the chicken and the egg; through delegation subordinates are trained, until they are trained jobs cannot be delegated. If the manager's assessment of his staff and the nature of the task are accurate, there should be no problems. You would not send a boy to do a man's job, it is the others who do that. It is not you who delegates the formulation of rush-hour traffic plans to the man who arrived in town yesterday. Lack of expertise may be as simple as lack of local knowledge. Usually it is the lack of professional or managerial skill. Delegation should be used to increase that skill, to test the basic job performance is sound, to broaden and develop experience, to stretch imagination. In delegating the task of checking hotel registers, a subordinate will have to understand something of Alien Registration, and not everyone's expert at that. A task will have been delegated which requires persistence, tact, descretion, a certain amount of record-keeping and record scrutiny. It should be delegated to someone ready for a minor task involving all those. For something more complex, like a detailed study of beats, someone is needed who can draw conclusions from figures, who can interpret trends and events, who has a sound knowledge of police organisation and procedures. Give it to someone without those, and what do you think the likely result will be? These skills may be present, though they have never been exercised before. Imagination is not stretched by performing the same task day after day, however complex that task may be.

From looking at the main errors, the three factors of delegation can be stated:

1. The Manager assigns clear tasks
2. The manager gives authority to make commitments, to use resources, to take action necessary to complete the task.
3. The manager creates an obligation for the satisfactory performance of the task.

Sometimes, the tasks you wish to delegate have been delegated to you, how then do you stand? There is generally no objection unless the task was intended for you personally, or it involves some legal procedure where authority cannot be transferred. Your task then becomes to see that someone else completes what was delegated to you, although you are still accountable to your superior for its completion. The same principle applies when you delegate parts of your delegated task, and you put them all together at the end. However, there are dangers

Delegation can operate on the chain principle, though a long chain causes problems of communication, of control and reference back, of transference of authority. The chain may induce too many bosses, the further away from the originator, the more the subordinate wonders exactly who he is working for, to whom he is accountable, particularly if the immediate superior merely pushes things up and own the chain. It becomes tempting to miss out a link or two and get on with the job, the result being that managers become accountable for something they know nothing about and responsible for a subordinate dealing direct with someone else. Re-delegation can and does work as long as the responsibilities and accountabilities are understood, and the temptation to by-pass them is resisted. Not everyone can resist temptation.

If delegation is so important, you may be wondering why it is not used more, why is there such a fuss if it delivers what it promises? The true test of leadership has been called simply the ability to delegate. Without reflecting on the glowing examples of history, you will learn by looking at the people you've worked with, and deciding in your own opinion the relationship between leadership and delegation. It will help to look at some attitudes towards it.

There are those who find it easy to delegate authority while remaining aware they cannot shed the responsibility. It is this awareness which allows them to delegate sensibly before their own work load becomes too great.

There are those who will delegate responsibility, but not authority. Keeping authority to themselves feeds their vanity, and they're hungry people. To give away authority is like parting with a piece of themselves, they think their stature is somehow diminished. In the eyes of their subordinates, the opposite is true. This type of manager often relies upon his rank because he has little else to offer. Another morsel for vanity is the delusion of indispensibility. No manager honestly believes that if he was promoted or dropped dead the job would stop, it has never happened before. And no one works twenty-four hours every day. It is a belief, like some other human failings which constantly denies the evidence of his own eyes, yet is firmly rooted. There is also the species who believes that because he can do everything better than anyone else, he alone must do it. If that belief is true, it points to a gross neglect of training. It also illustrates what he is denying his subordinates in skill and knowledge at the expense of ulcers and an early pension for his widow. Anyone who deludes themself to this extent is heading for the ultimate vanity, the head shrinkers couch.

The most formidable of all is the manager who can't delegate because he has not the managerial tools, he cannot communicate, he cannot organise, he cannot train, he cannot utilise the abilities of others. Forced by pressure of work to go through the motions of delegation, he does not pass enough information, he will not let go authority. Sometimes he does not trust his subordinates enough, he is not equipped to withstand situations where he has to rely on them, there is enough of those already for his harrassed brain to deal with. So, when he can cope, his subordinates have little to do. When he is pressed it is panic stations, jobs are thrown about willy-nilly, subordinates get the blame for those done badly. This type of manager put things off as long as possible because they are overworked through their own fault, they pick on the easy routine jobs, the very ones they should be delegating, they loose their sense of priorities. The situation always catches up with them, usually much sooner than they expect.

So you're going to be manager type 1? what should you delegate? Only guidelines can be given, not a comprehensive list. You know the circumstances, the timing, your men, you can predict the outcome, you will have to work it out for yourself.

a) *Tasks which subordinates can do as well as you,* the run of the mill and the slightly off key. You may suffer from delusions, your subordinates will not, even though they sit back and let you get on with it. Who is going to manage if you're involved in detail the newest recruit could handle? If you do their work, they may think you do not trust them. If the captain's below stoking the boilers, the crew may wonder who's steering the ship. Full steam ahead into the rocks is still a disaster.

b) *Tasks which require specialised abilities* you may not possess yourself, perhaps the assessment of accident black spots or the survey of buildings for crime risks. This does not mean giving the task to specialist officers necessarily, in any case you should not delegate to them unless you have responsibility for them and they are accountable to you. If one of your subordinates has spent time in traffic recently, it is possible that his knowledge is better than yours. It does not strike at your position as manager to acknowledge it, and having acknowledged it you would be foolish not to use it.

c) *Tasks which give subordinates experience.* This is covered in greater depth in the chapter on training. Suffice it here to say that men learn by doing, not by admiring the way you do it. It would be heart-warming if you were indispensible, your real role is to see the job goes on as well when you are not there as when you are, so it pays to make sure they can do it properly while you are present to control their efforts. That way you build confidence, broaden knowledge and experience. And lighten your own burden.

d) *Tasks which test abilities.* There is a lot who can talk a good fight, there's many who can weave a magic carpet of words, there is more than a few modest wallflowers who hide their true ability. You can forecast if your subordinates will be equal to a task, and you may be right. You may also be wrong, horses for courses are not always recognised until they have passed the post. If you are thinking of putting your shirt on one, it is better to try him over the distance first.

It will come as no surprise that there are some jobs which should not be delegated. Although obvious, they are worth repeating.

a) Some tasks will have been given to you personally, and not by virtue of your position as a manager, perhaps a task where the authority cannot be transferred because of a legal rule or an implied organisational procedure, for example, the detention of juveniles.

b) Those tasks where your skill and knowledge are essential. Take heart, you who frowned when it was stated earlier that the manager is rarely the only one who can do the job. There are still some jobs where your expertise is essential. It is for you to decide honestly what they are.

c) There will be occasions when, without bending the rules, you use your discretion to arrive at some acceptable, if slightly unusual solution. You may short cut through the organisational chain, you may decide that Standing Orders are inappropriate. On these decisions you stand or fall. Don't expect subordinates to take the same position, the consequences may be more severe for them.

d) Assessment of subordinates and discipline are such personal subjects, they need the personal touch. This does not mean a sergeant has no responsibility, it is his personally, even though the sergeant and inspector disagree. An inspector cannot leave it all to the sergeant under the excuse that he has delegated, the accusations of hiding behind someone are easily made. Delegation is not intended to pass off unpopular jobs.

e) All your work. Sitting relaxed behind an empty desk while subordinates rush about is not delegation, it is a sign you have misused your judgment. Delegation is a useful tool, it should be fitted to some purpose. Though you still have to manage your section, which is more than just keeping an eye on things, there's nothing to stop you doing certain jobs when they're swamped. Delegation should keep you from getting bogged down so much that you can't plan, organise, control manage; it will not stop you getting your hands dirty.

All this supposes that subordinates are waiting for nothing else than delegated tasks to fall in their laps, and you know that some of them are unwilling to accept any task. Some managers would dismiss them as lazy, incompetent, disinterested. Not you, you will look for reasons, and you may find them among the following: The victim of bad delegation. Once bitten a subordinate is twice shy. You may need to coax him, convince him by demonstrating that good delegation works, and is rewarding in terms of job satisfaction.

The victim of bad communication. You have done your best, but he still does not know what is expected of him. There's a barrier somewhere, usually connected with one of the other reasons.

The victim of overwork. Some men are overworked, reluctance to accept more is understandable. Usually these men are the good ones, the trusted ones. Even they expect work to be shared, it is not only camels who suffer strained backs from what appears a tiny straw.

The victim of self confidence. Not everyone has the confidence in himself that you have in him. If delegation is used to extend them, it is natural they should wonder if they can cope. Paradoxically, the only way to prove their ability is to do the job they don't think they can do.

The victim of restrictive leadership. Men who receive criticism for every mistake are unlikely to accept situations where the risks are increased.

The victim of bad training. Men who have been taught to rely on others for decisions, who find it easier to ask for instructions then work out solutions, the men without opinions who have been institutionalised.

The victim of genuine inability. There are some jobs which certain people just can not do, perhaps because they have not the knowledge or find it impossible to acquire. No one accepts tasks where they feel they are destined to make fools of themselves.

Often the reluctance to accept delegation is a combination of several reasons. It needs tact and patience to find the right ones, and until you've done that, you will not delegate with a quiet mind. Remembering that the responsibility is always yours, you will be tempted to be restrictive, to interfere, to do the job yourself. And that way, you will add more names to the victims of delegation.

So, once you've learnt the art of delegation, it is all plain sailing? You guessed, No. There is a risk, your subordinates are going to make mistakes, and you are going to be responsible for them. Some of the mistakes you will absorb, that is part of the burden you bear. People only develop as decision-makers by making decisions, seeing them implemented, considering the consequences. Everyone, from the comfort of their front room offering free advice to the television, can do better than the Prime Minister. Developing individuals means letting them feel the weight of authority and responsibility. They are not going to get it right first time every time. Someone took the brunt of your mistakes, even though you do not remember now. Too often the excuse for not delegating is the fear of what might happen. It does not hold good; if subordinates cannot be trusted nor trained, if any organisation sets itself such a standard that mistakes cannot be tolerated, there's something wrong with that organisation, and its managers.

8 Assessment & Appraisal

Promises, promises

Some day, on every manager's desk will flutter an intricate form with a grandiose name like "staff appraisal" or "personnel development report". This is the formal report to the organisation about the manager's subordinates. Like everything else a manager does, it should have some purpose, so the organisation takes it quite for granted that the ability to assess and appraise was in the same packet as the badges of rank received on promotion. After all, interviewing comes naturally, the capacity to weigh up other people is part of the policeman's trade; and what every policeman can do with rapists and burglars he can surely do with subordinates

To many managers the truth is different. Aware that the future of subordinates may be in their hands, they want to be fair both to the organisation and the subordinate, for in a good appraisal scheme their interests are identical, both want the right people in the right places at the right time. Yet the manager's judgement is delivered against no accurate measure, a man's past and future disposed of by ticks in boxes from a person with no training on how it should be done, who never interviewed anybody except witnesses and suspects, and who may be unsure what happens when the form leaves his desk. Will anyone read it if there's no inordinate vice disclosed, or will it meander through the usual channels to the personal file, there to rest midst the sick forms and the leave applications until the annual event recurs? Then perhaps, watch out. If the fellow's worse by a single tick, it's somebody's fault.

Every manager hopes he was assessed before he was elevated, though it may be that his memories of the process are not happy ones — a small comfort to most people that just whatever it was got them the job, it was not an objective assessment of their ability. Most managers know, or guess, they are being assessed now, though they may not know why, or how, or by who — all they suspect is somewhere there are bits of paper about them, possible blots on a career, pigeon holed until they are needed.

Human resources are the most vital, and probably the most expensive in any organisation; some means of communication upwards about them is vital for present performance to be monitored and future planning undertaken. Any scheme, by whatever name it is dubbed should fulfil both these functions because it deals with the performance of people within the organisation; it illuminates areas of weakness and strength enabling people to be put where their best talents are utilised, where they get the most satisfaction, where they can widen their experience or be trained to improve their performance, where careers can be planned. It gives those being appraised and assessed a chance to say what they think, what they want from the organisation as well as what they can contribute. It can give subordinates a sense of belonging, of knowing where he fits in a complicated pattern, that his contribution is being recognised and recorded, that he counts. Maybe it is those at the top who have the power to act — they cannot know everyone well enough to decide, and need to rely on accurate firsthand up-to-date knowledge from those who do, who observe free from prejudice and bias.

Put all together, the forms accurately and honestly completed in a trusted system can point out flaws in the organisational structure, show where policies are misdirected. Maybe that sergeant was right, he has too much responsibility, he has too many men to control. Maybe that constable was right, the new housing estate in the middle of the beat unchanged for 90 years has grown too much for one man when compared with all the others in the division. Indeed, some would claim a flawless system tells senior management a lot of what it needs to know about how it's doing. But before that, those on the ground, the appraisers and the appraised, the assessors and the assessed must know all they need to know about the system itself.

To put things in perspective, there are three prerequisites of any assesment and appraisal system: a job analysis, a job description and a job specification. In the police service they are rarely used. It is said that it is impossible to formulate any of them. In this context, impossible means difficult, which is not quite the same. In fact they are used, but unscientifically, personal opinion substituting for observable fact. To understand assessment, any manager must know the measure against which he is assessing. That is what the analytical approach provides. In its absence, every manager provides his own measure, even unconsciously, when he separates his sheep and goats. He will assess against the

pedigree ram, because all assessment is a comparison with some ideal. It does not need spelling out what the effects can be in a system where each manager has to determine if the ideal pedigree has long or short wool, that horns are unnecessary or desirable, that good mutton is lean or fatty or somewhere in between. JOB ANALYSIS Before anyone can arrive at a sensible decision about whether a person is qualified to do any job, or whether they are doing that job well, it is necessary to have a clear statement of what the job is. Obvious, of course; though how many job analyses have you seen about the policeman? It depends not just on rank, but what post an individual occupies, and therefore an analysis must be made of each job in the organisation, Divisional Detective Inspector, Detective Inspector in the Regional Crime Squad, Task Force Detective Inspector, Detective Inspector in the Record Office. This is the analysis of the job itself, not the person doing it at the moment. The techniques used will differ according to the nature of the job, in industry repetitive manual jobs are analysed by work study; supervisory jobs are analysed by studying the organisational structure, the responsibilities, talking to the present holder of the post and his immediate superiors. Which ever method or combination of methods is used, the information obtained should set out the nature of the job exactly. This becomes the job description.
JOB DESCRIPTION is a statement of the purpose, responsibilities and tasks which comprise a job. It starts off with a title to identify the job within the organisation. Then follows the list of duties and responsibilities which should be as precise as possible although in fields such as the use of discretion and initiative it is impossible to be exhaustive. Next come the skills and knowledge demanded by the job, for instance a traffic sergeant must be able to drive a car and have a working knowledge of traffic legislation. The working environment is included, outdoors or inside, alone or with others, from one place or different places as in the case of an inspector in a subdivision with several stations. Finally, there may be added the rates of pay and allowances for the job, plain clothes, car allowance, regular overtime without option. Below is a specimen job description, sufficient to illustrate how they are drawn up. It is not exhaustive.

Job Title   : Traffic Inspector, "A" Division.

Responsibilities   : *To Chief Superintendent "A" Division:*
and Duties   Investigation of all accidents within division.

Recommendation for process of all offences arising from accidents.

Arranging supplies of fuel, oil and category 1 spares for all vehicles in the division.

Supervision of all traffic personnel in the division.

To Chief Superintendent Road Traffic:
Assessment of traffic management schemes within division however initiated.

Care and custody of road traffic vehicles.

Recommendations for driver training.

Organisation of Road Safety within division.

Skills and Knowledge

Advanced driver.

Thorough working knowledge of traffic legislation.

Ability to examine motor vehicles for defects.

Ability to plan work load for a section of three sergeants and 23 constables.

Ability to supervise above.

Working Conditions : Irregular hours with occasional overtime. Supervision of traffic patrols on duty and attendance at incidents necessary in all weathers.

Telephone provided.

From the job description comes the job specification, sometimes called the man or personnel specification, which sets out the type of person needed to do the job satisfactorily. To some extent, this is always an ideal, the best person in every respect may be hard to find, and if the appointment is limited to within the organisation itself, then it is the best available. Of course, training and experience can be supplied to improve the actual towards the ideal. The job specification also sets down the qualifications and personality required. There is some overlapping between the specification and description in the area of qualifications. Job specifications are used to measure people doing one sort of work with others so that their skill and experience are developed for the health of the organisation and the satisfaction of the people who make it up. Below is a specimen job description. Again it sets out only enough to show the layout, it is not intended to be complete.

Job Title	: Traffic Inspector "A" Division.
Qualifications	: Promotion Examination to Inspector Advanced driving certificate, Class I Age between 26 and 50 years. Male or female.
Experience	: At least two years. traffic work in any rank. At least two years experience of supervising operational police officers.
Qualities	Ability to lead and generate enthusiasm amongst a section of experienced men. Even-tempered, yet firm. Able to withstand public criticism of the work of his department, including public discussion. A belief in the importance of both education and prosecution as means of enforcing driver discipline. An interest in motor vehicles.

Only those qualifications and qualities which are necessary should be listed. Many people will have others which are irrelevant unless they are a positive obstacle to satisfactory job performance. For instance, a degree in mechanical engineering is not required, though it would be useful. A Traffic Inspector who believes that the use of radar is unfair, as many motorists claim, is unlikely to give his section the leadership it has the right to expect in the use of this equipment. A Traffic Inspector who cannot keep his temper in the sight of bad driving is unlikely to initiate a spirit of education among his section. However, only those qualities which are essential, or positive obstacles, should be set down, otherwise the task of finding the paragon to fit the thousands of desirable virtues will be impossible.

The examples above set out the system in outline only. Each organisation designs the detail to suit the tasks it carries out and the type of people it needs. It is enough to appreciate the part played by each initially, as the basis for the planned selections system when taking on new staff or transferring within the organisation. And if you have not got them in your organisation, someone must have more than a fair idea of them for each job, otherwise assessment and appraisal become so much waste paper, and round pegs in round holes a matter of chance. If you've never seen them, ask. And as a management exercise, write out those for your immediate subordinates. One word of caution before you reach for your pen, it is the job, not how *he* does it: it is the ideal person not *him*. When you've got the hang of it, you may find your assessment and appraisal become more objective, less a personal opinion tossed out in the early hours of the morning as just another form to fill in.

The words assessment and appraisal are used indiscriminately, whatever meaning is attached to them in any organisation, that's what the managers should mean when they use them. Specifically, assessment is about individuals, their personalities, their qualities, abilities, what motivates them, how all these may be enhanced by training. Appraisal in the measurement of a person's performance against the job description. The connection between the two is so close that it is difficult to consider one without the other. Any manager who can keep the two separate in his mind starts with an advantage. Assessment is what a man is: appraisal how he works. Consideration of one, why he does not make enough arrests (appraisal) will often indicate something about the other, lacks physical courage (assessment).

Selection is only the start of a career, or a change within a career structure. Everyone has to grow into a new job, during this period comparisons with predecessors or expectations of the quick attainment of full stature without time for growth, are unhelpful. Until people are familiar with their working environment, which includes a change of office as well as a change of job, they will not perform to full capacity. A simple example is the constable posted to a new section, he will not be at his best until he has learnt the beats and the "common knowledge" about them.

In a sense, the shaking-down period is a time of weakness for the individual. The speed with which he adapts may be a strength, and is capable of assessment. Constables will be watched to see how they are making out. This is assessment by the sergeant and inspector, and will be carried on until they are satisfied that the new members of the section have settled down in their work situation. Then many managers relax their assessment, on the assumption that the absence of trouble means all is well. This may not be so at all, there can be all sorts of doubts and difficulties which are real to the constable if not apparent to others, even simple things like which form to fill in, the policy on verbal cautions for motoring offences. The man who is always asking questions is sometimes regarded worse than the man who says nothing, and that's no secret. If assessment has stopped, there will be no difference to the manager between the man who does not know and the man who does not care. The relaxation also indicates that satisfactory job performance has been achieved, that the nature of the job remains unchanged, and that a minimum standard is set. Assessment is a continuing process; a manager who is not constantly assessing subordinates against the targets set is in no position to make an appraisal.

The higher the manager's position in the structure, the more people he will have to assess and appraise. If it is more than ten, there's more than an even chance he'll have forgotton the assessments he's made of each individual when he comes to the appraisal. You would not be the first to grade the worst fellow on the section as outstanding because you got him mixed up with someone else, or based it entirely on the one outstanding piece of work he performed in 12 months. There's no reason why any manager should not keep a notebook, twelve months is a long time to remember who's done what exactly, the different impressions they have made through the year, for no one reveals all his qualities and personality in one or two brief meetings. The notebook will keep the manager's mind on the targets he's set. A short note may remind the manager that the chap who got that marvellous write-up in the local paper did not deserve it because he acted in flagrant disregard of instructions, or that the young lad who's still not quite got it has much more of it than last year, and he's making a genuine effort.

Assessment is the consideration of many aspects of personality ability, intelligence, knowledge and skill. Some of these change, confidence for instance, may be lacking in new work situations, partly because of doubts about ability, partly because the new working group will be sounding the new man out, and he will be doing the same. How soon an individual adjusts to a new situation, what he is prepared to do to further that adjustment tells the manager something about the man. Knowledge should increase with experience, how soon that happens, if at all, indicates something about the man, his personality, his character, all the things that go to make him, him. Not everyone is boastful, not everyone is reticent, unless a formal qualification is accepted as proof, there is no accurate test of a person's ability to do the job, other than letting him do it and observing his approach. Among other things, this should show his social skills, if he gets on with other people, and if not, why, some people establish relationships quicker than others, some offer a hand, others wait for the world to come to them. It will show if he's got drive to carry out the job, some jobs require more of it than others, often drive that carries others along. It will show if he can lead, if he cooperates with his mates or if self-seeking, willing to build his career at other's expense. Can he make decisions, yet seek advice when he needs to; is he reliable, does the work get done as a matter of course, or is it last-minute, hasty and sketchy, indicating he doesn't plan far ahead.

The good manager through continual assessment will establish what motivates his people in their ego needs, and this again will show something about their characters and personality. The man who constantly seeks praise, even at the expense of others, reveals something about himself to the manager who is looking. The manager who stopped assessing when the subordinate had been in the job a few weeks will have little revealed to him.

Naturally, managers who work in close proximity to their people won't wait until the annual "let's see how you've been doing", they'll have taken action offering advice, encouragement and praise, reprimanding intelligently. They will also have noted the response. Some people resent advice, take reprimands badly, and it shows, to the extent sometimes that the advice is deliberately ignored, or in extreme cases that the exact opposite is done in an attempt to establish independence.

The closer a manager works with people, the more involved he becomes with them personally; there's always the temptation to draw back from criticism because of hurt feelings, retaliation, a heavy air in the office. Criticism can be made as nicely as the manager knows how, it still happens. So it's all saved up for the annual appraisal, then there's words like "stab in the back", "bad faith and betrayal", "you never said anything at the time". These wounds leave permanent scars, a well-deserved rebuke at the time soon heals. This is why continuing assessment is vital, the appraisal gives both manager and managed opportunities that don't occur every day, a more detached opportunity for both to speak their minds. Some managers feel that working almost shoulder-to-shoulder with subordinates, they know them well enough to dispense with appraisal, and the interview. What those managers don't know, and what they can't know is whether the subordinate wants an appraisal because there's something on his mind, or because he wants confirmation of his general impression of what his manager thinks about him, deduced soley from the number of times he's been reprimanded in the past months. And he's a right to know.

On continuous assessment may be based solicited recommendations for promotion, transfers to fill the eternal gaps in C.I.D. strength, someone to look after that loveable furry creature just added to the dog section. The closer the manager to those he assesses, the more opportunities for accurate assessment. It is the immediate manager who should know his people best, it is his judgement which should be the crucial one, it is his responsibility to develop his subordinates. Assessment is the only way it can be done accurately; numbers may be drawn out of the hat, favourites may be speeded on their way, the manager's reward is that he still has to manage those who really did deserve it, and everyone knows.

Appraisal will be carried out as the policy of each organisation determines, each has its own time scale, type of form, method of determination and nomination of appraisers. Some require information about job performance only. Some are assessment schemes concerned with the personality and qualities of individuals. Many are a mixture of both, though whether that is intended is often open to conjecture. For the sake of clarity, appraisal will be used here to cover all of them.

Whatever the scheme, one thing they have in common is a scale of assessment. The descriptive scale gives a series of qualities together with a list of gradings, say between outstanding and poor. The correct grading is indicated by a mark in the appropriate box. Some scales show the extremes between which the grading is made, e.g. from completely dependable to unreliable. Others spell out the gradings, specifying the gradual build up from the worst to the best e.g. Unreliable at all times, sometimes reliable, usually reliable, unreliability is an exception, always reliable.

The number of gradings is usually an odd number between seven and three; the greater the choice, in theory the greater the accuracy and for the manager, the harder the task in fixing the correct point across the scale. The higher the number of gradings, the greater the precision required in determining the difference between good and very good, and the more open it becomes to the manager's subjective interpretation.

The numerical scale is similar to the descriptive, except it uses numbers instead of descriptive gradings. Like the descriptive scales, the numbers vary between three and seven, with the uneven middle number representing average. In numerical scales totals can be made; a minimum number is sometimes set to represent satisfactory job performance. Care is needed, this may give an inaccurate overall assessment: if there are ten areas of appraisal, each scaled from 1 to 5, and the minimum for satisfactory performance is 20, anyone who scores the maximum on four areas of performance will achieve the minimum; he need not score at all on the remaining six.

A variation on the numerical scale is the diagraminatic scale. The various areas of appraisal are numbered, then radiate from a central point like the spoke of a wheel. The job standard is traced by linking the spokes at the rim of the wheel, and the measurement of people superimposed. At a glance it can be seen where differences occur. This technique is more often used in staff selection, but it is useful for appraisal in indicating areas of strength and weakness.

Whatever system is used, unless based on scientifically-measureable results, it depends on the subjective judgement of managers who, being human, are prone to error. Some of them may be a misinterpretation of the system. Others may be because of the meaning of words. Loyalty often appears as a quality to be commented upon. What is it? To whom does it lie? Is a subordinate sometimes critical of the organisation disloyal? Those who have the interests of the organisation at heart may feel its ills and wish to cure them. Is such a person less loyal than those who take the organisation with blind obedience or dumb indifference? Does trustworthiness refer to keeping fingers out of the petty cash, keeping silent about confidential matters or doing what is directed without supervision? These vague words mean different things to different managers and subordinates. The point is simple, unless the appraiser knows the exact meaning of the abstract words for his organisation, he can be neither fair nor accurate. Not too bad perhaps when he's the only one playing the game, though in big organisations where each manager puts his interpretation of the abstract as the correct one, some of the results are not hard to forecast.

Appraisal does reflect the appraiser. If the manager believes that beards are untidy or unnecessary, the clean-shaven may be one grade up on the hirsute in the cleanliness bearing and turnout box, although the fellow with the neatly trimmed beard may be cleaner better turned out than those with untidy short hair. And from this, its not too big a step to assume that because the manager doesn't like beards, the hairy ones can not be interested in the job, are disloyal and disobedient. All managers have prejudices, the most dangerous are those they themselves are unaware of. Known or unknown, personal prejudice has no place in appraisal, and it is the easiest of traps to walk into. Prejudice leads to distorted appraisal, the following were written by two inspectors about the same constable, based on the same degree of knowledge and the same facts. There is no prize for guessing which the constable preferred, the interesting point is which was accurate, or were they both saying the same thing, filtered through prejudice.

He has a mind of his own and an enquiring attitude.

He shows some originality and thinks for himself.

He may develop valuable qualities of leadership.

He can be insubordinate and question the decisions of those in authority.

He is argumentative and apt to be obstinate.

He may become a bad influence.

There is no doubt that those comments by different people on the same facts indicate as much about the makers as about the man himself.

Another pitfall is to assume too much from one event, proof based on too little evidence. Some men will make a catastrophic mistake or work a miracle. They'll be remembered for that, perhaps the folklore of the service through it. It should be taken into account in any appraisal, though not at the expense of everything else they have done in the past year. Everyone makes mistakes, even managers. The old saw that the man who never made a mistake never made anything is true; it is also true that the more a man does the more mistakes he is likely to make. Mistakes shouldn't be hung round people's necks for the rest of their careers because some manager was too lazy or unskilled to see them in perspective. Similarly with the miracle workers, they can't coast along for ever on the one occasion they changed water to wine. Hanging everything on one event is the sign of the manager who doesn't know his people.

There is something in the ethics of modern organisations which demands that each space on a form must be filled. Whatever scale of assessment is used, there may be questions which a manager cannot answer and the subordinate is reluctant to do so, because the type of job has not been carried out or there is insufficient evidence on which to appraise. Leadership is a quality on which managers are asked to pronounce, yet does everyone get a chance to display it? A constable working a detached beat may have no one to lead but himself, telling the public what to do isn't leadership. Relations with colleagues is another difficult one to answer, the manager may observe, but he is not a member of the working group, and his observations may point him in the wrong direction. On any areas of appraisal where the manager feels that he cannot appraise, he should say so, resisting the temptation to mark "average" as the way of saving face. The man may be appalling, he may be outstanding; the manager who does not know should have the courage to say so.

Finally, back to those vague abstractions like initiative and judgement. These can only be assessed where there is evidence from the job performance that good or bad judgement has been exercised in specific instances; it is not the manager's opinion that a person has or has not judgement which is required. Most people exercise it well on some occasions, not so well on others. It is which side the balance tips that counts.

Unless the scheme asks for it, future potential is not part of appraisal, which is the man's job performance based on determined results and the qualities he brings to doing that job. Any manager at the end of appraisal may make recommendations for training, or extending experience to mitigate weakness and strengthen strength. Too often the manager's opinion that Peter Plod will make a good dog-handler defeats an accurate appraisal of Peter Plod's performance, assuming that if the dog handler's job does not come along it will be the end of the world.

No manager can make an accurate appraisal without discussing it with the person he's appraising. There's enough suspicion about any reporting system without creating more. The person appraised has the right to be told honestly what that appraisal is, he is right to correct the misconceptions, he is right to battle with the manager's prejudice, he is right to test the evidence on which conclusions are based. The best proof that the rights have been granted is the person's initials on the appraisal. They don't mean that he agrees with it, they do mean that he has seen it, that the manager has courage and honesty. Appraisal is no part of the secret service.

Before considering appraisal interviews, it's worth clearing out of the way some of the things that they are not intended to be. They are not intended to establish if the person being interviewed is good enough to do the job. If he is not, it is the fault of the selection procedure. Managers are reluctant to put a bottom-of-the-scale appraisal, however honest, because they think it shows a man is incapable of doing the job. In a well-designed scheme it only shows there is much room for improvement. It is not intended that appraisal interviews should be the annual penance, in which the subordinate's sins and omissions receive a fresh raking over. Neither should they be marking exercises like football pools. Managers who pick winners without discussion richly deserve the attitude that will be adopted towards them and their appraisal scheme.

An appraisal interview requires preparation, it should not be done off the cuff when the manager finds a few minutes he can't otherwise fill. The essential part of the preparation is to ensure that both appraiser and appraised understand its purpose and the form it will take. This gives the appraised the chance to think about it, perhaps make a few notes of his own so he won't be taken by surprise when the manager starts talking about something long-forgotten. Both need to know:-

a) Why the scheme exists, its objectives, the wisdom of identifying training needs and enlarged experience, in relation to the effective management of the organisation.

b) What factors will be reviewed, what scales of assessment are used, what records of the interview will be made.

c) The relationship to promotion, whether the scheme is based on potential as well as performance.

d) How any recommendations will be implemented, whether the manager has the authority to carry them out or put them in the hands of someone else.

This information should be given to the appraised before the interview. Taking him by surprise or confronting him in a position of ignorance may put him on the defensive when the purpose of the interview is to promote a two-way discussion.

A manager needs time to prepare and plan his interview, to collect information from the records of the people to be interviewed in support of what will be said about the standard of job performance. Failure to take these preliminary steps results in no feed back, no rapport and a bad interview. When the preparations have been made, enough time for the interview should be set aside and privacy guaranteed.

Any subordinate comes to an appraisal interview wondering how its going to turn out, hoping for the best while half expecting the worst; the first essential is to put him at his ease. This proves difficult if the manager insists the subordinate stands while he sits, or the chair is set in the formal sit to attention position. Managers have to bear in mind that their rank is a barrier to communication, and do their best to surmount it. Getting off the manager's own ground on to neutral territory helps, provided uninterrupted privacy can be guaranteed.

Satisfied with the arrangements for the interview, the manager should open it with a brief review of the appraised's work in progress. It helps to begin in an area where satisfaction can be expressed, and everyone has such areas, no one is that hopeless. Satisfaction relaxes the appraised, encourages them to talk. During the interview the appraised may hint at some of his weaker points, giving the manager the chance to probe and establish whether the problem lies with the individual or the organisation.

Probing is a technique which requires practice. In essence, it is the technique used to get information from witnesses. Probing questions begin with "why" "how" "what" "tell me about" "in what way do you", questions which can't be answered by a simple "yes" or "no", questions which tell the interviewer what he wants to know. The answers should be followed up until the interviewer is satisfied he understands not just what happened, but why it happened, not only what a man thinks, but why he thinks that. In addition, and no less important, the interview itself will run smoother with less gaps, less awkward silences.

The test of a probing interview is who has done the talking. If it was 20% interviewer, 80% interviewed, it was probably a probing one. If the figures are the other way round, was it an interview or a lecture.

One man was asked if he had enjoyed working in the divisional office as part of his training. He replied "no" and the manager passed onto the next question, making a mental note that this chap was not the stuff from which divisional clerks are made.

Had the manager persued the aversion to the divisional office, he would have learnt that his man's time there coincided with the new clothing issue, and for a fortnight, all he had done was parcel up new uniform and sort through old. He felt he had been used as a pair of hands, that he had never worked in the divisional office as such, he wanted to find out what happened there and felt let down because he'd been stuck with the annual rag trade. In fact, that man had all the makings of a good divisional office clerk.

For success in a probing interview, more is required of the manager than the interviewee. Wholesome sympathy, patience and understanding must be evident. However unusual the answers to your questions, even those you know are nonsense, accept them calmly, do not explode in half strangled expletives. If he is genuine in what he says — his point of view, however misguided, determines what he does and why he does it. Aggressive questions will be met with defensive answers, or hostility if he believes attack is the best form of defence, and it is his interpretation of the question which counts; to him, your little joke meant to put him at ease such as "How did you like being the office man, drank a lot of tea I suppose?" reveals what you think about office men, and he will start to defend himself, "No more than anyone else," which may be true, but does not answer the questions you asked. Similarly, leading questions are unhelpful because they do not bring out the information. "There's not much difficulty with the new crime reports, is there?" is more a statement than a question, and will invariably be answered as suggested. Such questions can easily indicate an appraisal already made, a mind already made up, so there's not much point in discussing the subject.

If the appraised does not mention his weaker points, and many will not even if the phone does not keep ringing and people do not keep popping in and out, and they do trust the person appraising them, the manager must. It is vital this is done in a constructive way, backed up by supportive evidence. As in court, hearsay has no part in appraisal interviews, and for the same reasons, its accuracy cannot be determined to the satisfaction of the parties concerned. In discussing areas of weak performance, expect people to go onto the defensive (a perfectly human reaction; no one likes to confess their inadequacies) but it is vital the manager understands them and can get an acknowledgement of them. A sin confessed is half way absolved. Success in this area depends on how the appraised looks at his manager, whether as leader, counsellor, adviser, or as judge about to don the black cap. An explanation of the appraisal objective will often encourage a constructive point of view on both sides. If the manager has an obligation to provide training or increase experience, (as opposed to making recommendations to some one else) this is the time to spell out how it's to be done. But do not make false promises, you are just as much a prisoner of your appraisal system as the chap on the other side of the desk, do not pretend your power is greater than it really is. If you can, this is the time to set targets for better job performance, and a man is more likely to reach for them if he feels he's had a fair say in making them realistic. Once they've been agreed, arrangements can be made about feedback on progress. It may be improving the standard of written reports to be monitored over the next six months with you helping on certain types of report; it may be knocking the abrasive edge from a brusque approach to the customers; it may be a lack of knowledge on one aspect of law.

Avoid ending the interview on a discordant note. The appraised should leave feeling that he has been fairly appraised, that he has had the opportunity to say his piece, to ask questions and receive answers from someone prepared to sit and listen, that the things which are causing him concern have been dealt with as well as those troubling the manager. Ending on a discordant note colours the entire interview that way, for both parties.

It is better to take notes during the interview than waiting until the man has left the room, and if the appraised is doing most of the talking, the manager has time. There's no need to conceal what's going on, the purpose of the appraisal should be known, the appraised may be curious as to what is being written, he will be curious to the point of suspicion if the manager pretends he is not note-taking. Notes are helpful when the form comes to be completed, they clarify the thoughts, they help to pick precisely the right box for all those ticks, and one man can be compared with another as some appraisal systems require. Besides, any manager who does more than one interview in the same afternoon will have forgotten some of the points made by the first fellow by the time he has finished with the third.

When it comes to filling in the form, be honest, be accurate, have courage. Resist the temptation to up-grade because a bad appraisal reflects on you, the manager, and resist the same temptation because good gradings prove how well you're doing your job. Resist the temptation to mark average because you can't be bothered to sort it out accurately, or to fail to mark the "excellents" in case they let you down.

Because interviewing is a human activity, it does not always run smoothly, though many of the pitfalls will be removed by careful preparation. There will be encounters where the appraised comes to the interview in the wrong frame of mind, particularly if previous sorties have been unpleasant. It is vital for the interviewer not to get caught up in the situation, returning like for like. The object is not to win a battle nor get the better of an argument, it is to communicate, an unlikely occurrence where barriers of agression are thrown up on both sides. It will sometimes help if the appraiser can keep the interview on uncontroversial ground until he senses that the agression has evaporated, for often, that agression is no more than a demonstration of uncertainty.

Another appraisal difficulty is the person who won't stop talking. He sees the interview as his opportunity to spell everything out in minute detail, making extensive suggestions for his future, and seeking a firm commitment that those suggestions will be implemented. It is tempting to shut this person up, though that will only confirm any suspicions he may harbour that he will not be allowed his say. A planned interview will give him some leeway, he will have his say while the interview travels along the route picked by the appraiser.

More difficult is the person who says nothing, except the occasional grunt when asked a direct question. Possibly this reticence is based on a misunderstanding of the purpose of appraisal, or a simple mistrust of the system. Knowing the cause of the reticence will indicate the way of breaking it down, although mistrust is not overcome in five minutes. Skillful probing on uncontroversially ground will usually loosen rigid tongues.

Knowledge of the people the manager controls helps in all appraisal interviews; if the appraised is acting in character the manager will have dealt with the problems before and should have structured the interview with them in mind; if the appraised is acting out of character patience and probing, plus an understanding of what the interview's about will usually bring the person back to form. Keeping on neutral ground until it happens helps.

Any manager is likely to be challenged to substantiate what has been said about the appraised, they should be prepared to keep their hackles down. Any man has a perfect right to ask how a particular conclusion about him has been arrived at, that's why it's important to have supporting evidence. To be challenged and be unable to prove the conclusions leaves the appraiser in a difficult position for the rest of the interview. And, when the news breaks on the grapevine, it may throw the appraisal system into disrepute with others. There are are always those, "agin" it anyway, willing to pour petrol on smouldering fires.

It is worth repeating that one of the major difficulties all managers face during the interview is keeping his own prejudices in order. Appraisal schemes are for the good of the organisation, not the manager. He is only the tool used to ensure the best is obtained from the manpower available. There are from the organisation's point of view neither good nor bad appraisals, only accurate and inaccurate ones.

Having filled in the form, it has been said that the subordinate should see it. If the manager wants time to consider, he should take it, though that is not an excuse for denying people the chance to see their appraisal. It does not build up trust in a system to produce a completed form before the interviewer has given them a chance to say their piece. Nor does it build up trust to deny them the chance to see what has been written. People will not agree with everything that's been said; if they don't know what's been said and things happen afterwards unconnected in fact with the appraisal, but in their minds resulting from it, they'll never believe the manager's protestations unless they've the evidence of their own eyes.

The responsibility does not end with putting the completed form in the out tray and breathing a sigh of relief. Any follow-up action such as training, increased delegation or broader experience should be arranged by the manager. If appraisal schemes have any value, they should be the basis on which the development of the individual is planned. Past performance is not a true guide to future performance, though it is better than a crystal ball, and often all that's available.

It defeats the system if nothing happens from well-conducted appraisals, to the subordinate it becomes just so much talk, just another form-filling exercise, a bit of propaganda to hide the disinterest of the organisation. And if that is the true picture, it will save time, money and everyone's temper to scrap the whole rigmarole and employ a clairvoyant, for a discredited appraisal system does more harm than no system at all.

9 Training

ONE AND ONE IS THREE

There is a widely-held view that the only place to train policemen is on the streets, "the University of the Pavements" for the copper's job is action, dealing with people, controlling situations. This view is misleading in its assumption that five years in "the University" will ensure all students graduate with the Diploma of Practical Coppering, thereafter becoming the mythical creature who stalks every police station – the practical policeman.

This creature knows no theory, he cannot pass exams, he is no good on paper; but if a job needs doing, he is the man, a wave of his arm restores traffic chaos to order, his presence quells riots, he charms thieves from their hiding places. Strangely, when you are the mythical creature's sergeant or inspector, he loses his appeal, the reports do not get submitted, there are always loose ends in what he does, he only tackles the routine he has done a thousand times before. And all his triumphs were in the past.

No one tells the practical man that he needs training, for he is experienced, and experienced men are sacred, despite the obvious truth that experience is not what happens to people, it is what they learn from what happens to them. "The University of the Pavements" needs its professors and lecturers to interpret knowledge and experience like any other; there must be students and teachers. As a manager, this academic post of distinction is one of the hats you wear. So if you're walking round with something on your head others can see, it's best you know what it is.

What about District Training Centres and Force Training Departments, you may be tempted to ask: training is a specialist function, not the job of sergeants and inspectors groaning under the weight of operational responsibilities – they 're too busy making sure the job gets done. The fallacy which the University promotes stems from treating theory and practice as separate watertight compartments instead of complementary and necessary means to the same end – the best standard of job performance. Training departments concentrate on theory for two reasons: they are equipped to teach it effectively, and they cannot teach practice.

They can teach the basis of statement taking, they can do no more than suggest the attitude to deal with the witness more interested in watching Z cars than telling the real live polite probationer what happened in the slight accident last Saturday. However well designed, role playing exercises have an air of unreality, it is inescapable. However good the instructor, underneath the shabby mac and intoxicated voice he is still the chap who drew the nice coloured chart about the Diseases of Animals Act.

Those same sergeants and inspectors who are too busy making sure the job gets done are the only people who can train effectively once the groundwork of theory has been laid; they alone can correct mistakes, shape attitudes, interpret events, marry all that theory to the daily business of police work. And their training role is more difficult — no nine to five days split into neat periods with a fistful of notes on what is to happen in each of them and tests every Friday to encourage effort and chart progress — they write their own syllabus from what is happening on the section, decided often as the event is occurring, and the examinations are doing the job itself with a demanding public and a busy super to mark the papers. Operational managers have neither the time nor the refinements of the specialist trainer, but they should have the same attitude towards it because their role is vital, and they are going to benefit from that attitude in many different ways, not least of which is the absence of nightmares.

"The University of the Pavement" seems to suggest that graduates don't need theory. It is fashionable to dismiss book learning and courses, particularly if you are no good at either. But if "the University" does not deal with theory, how does it teach its graduates to arrest for theft without defining what theft is? Intuition? Well, if you want to run a section on intuition . . . No one is suggesting that learning the subtle nuances of the law is easy, or that insight into human behaviour is the simplest of subjects. Nevertheless, every practical policeman needs some theory, some basis on which to start the undergraduate course, even if pride makes him deny it. As a manager, you need theory and practice for your self-respect, unless you do not care that young fellows with six months service know more about your job than you, or ask your subordinate for advice which you cannot give. You also need it for your acceptability.

"The University" trains by dropping people in at the deep end. No one has counted the fatalities, or those who breathlessly struggled to the side and slunk away, or those brave souls who went in time and time again when five minutes on the side would have taught them. "The University" only acknowledges successes, since it denies any inadequacy it has no reason for providing a better method. How many resources in terms of manpower and talent it has squandered is anyone's guess.

So let us get down to the "who", the "how", the "where", the "why", the "what" and the "when" of training.

The "who" is easily answered; managers have resources at their command, and the most valuable is manpower. Training develops this resource, lack of training wastes it. No one has suggested the raw recruit should be pushed into the cruel world without any training, why should the assumption prevail that all subordinates require no other training or guidance than what chance feeds to him? Even if they get the right experience, they may be hiding mistakes. The "who" is all subordinates, regardless of rank or experience.

The "why" should be obvious: to maintain and raise the standard of job performance for all subordinates, to prepare them for additional responsibility, to increase the efficiency of the organisation. In perpetual motion, organisations go forward or back, they don't stand still; like the dinosaur, the world in which they live changes and if they cannot adapt they stagger fretfully towards a painful extinction. And just another reminder, organisations are people. Safety is also a prime factor, training develops safe working habits which are not likely to be broken. This is important when it comes to building teamwork; it is the guy who goes his own sweet way at the crucial moment who wrecks the objective. You'll have seen it happen enough to do without an example.

The "when" is comparatively simple; training is a constant process, we really do learn a little something every day if we are eager to be taught, it is not reserved for the classroom. Knowledge for its own sake may have attractions, that's not a training objective and those who wish to possess such a treasure house should build it in their own time. This is not saying that a wide general knowledge may not be useful in all situations a policeman may meet, it is the difference between learning and learning to some purpose. Whenever a man learns in a classroom, it should be so that he can better do his job; whenever he is doing his job he should be learning from it. As manager, you should be making sure he does. One word of caution however, not all training may be relevant at the time it is carried out; a lot of police training is connected with what might happen. It is still training, you do not sink the ship to carry out boat drill. From this it follows that the "where" can be anywhere the job takes him, which is everywhere.

The "what" implies specific training objectives. These are not the pious "to be a good policeman" or "to do the job properly". There is a distinct relationship between training objectives and job satisfaction, although the latter is something the service does not write down very often, so the former are somewhat hazy. The organisation should say in precise terms what it requires of a constable, and if it does not you must interpret the general directions as best you can. If you think about it, you know the specifications in some detail, you know what is expected from your section or department, especially by you. Is a constable with six months' service expected to handle a company fraud from petty cash voucher to Crown Court? Is he expected to deal with a simple theft, preparing the file for court, including all those T.I.C's the prisoner's bursting to get off his chest? Should a constable be able to do a sudden death from expiration of breath to inquest on the day the full time Coroner's Officer is winning the Chief Constable's Golf Cup? On the day you are dazzling the promotion board, is your sergeant expected to submit all the reports or just some of them? Do you honestly demand the same from all your men irrespective of their experience and temperament? If the answer is negative, should not training be different for each individual according to the ascending standards you set? For in all the situations above, the words "deal", "handle" and "do" imply the right approach, the correct attitude, enough confidence and sufficient technique as well as the recognition of the precise offence and the use of the proper report.

Dealing with people, often when they are frightened, embarrassed or angry, needs considerable social skills — vital things like the right initial approach which sets the tone for the rest of the interview, the different ways of approaching different types of people, knowing when to talk and when to keep quiet, how to read a person's eyes to judge if questions are being pushed too hard, when a bit of humour will help and when it will cause offence. The often made assumption that these things come naturally, that people develop these skills intuitively, is wrong in many cases. Young policemen are taught they should be tolerant, but when, and where, and how? Their experiences need sorting our realistically; many people think they are being tolerant when to everyone else they are being everything but. Attitudes to people and what they do are important, social skills depend on them; there is a lot of evidence which shows people do not consciously work out attitudes for themselves, they copy those around them, particularly those they judge desirable. That judgment can sometimes be faulty.

And it is not just dealing with the public; social skills are needed to get along with their mates, and their managers. Your group will need to explain things to you, to argue their case, to persuade you, remaining polite as they say what they feel needs saying with some passion and sincerity. They will have to tell you, kindly, that you are wrong sometimes, or you are not getting across to them, a delicate situation for both sides. Taking for granted your willingness to listen, you will respond not just to what they say, but to the way that they say it.

Social skills are essential tools for the policeman's job, they need sharpening occasionally even after the apprentice has been taught to use them with all the skill of the craftsman.

In part, the "what" determines the "how". Training is more than the acquisition of knowledge, whether that be the ability to render a word-perfect recital of the Theft Act or the skill to complete the most obscure Home Office Stats form. You probably know the old Arabic proverb: In European script it reads "*ana asmaa ana ansa ana ara ana atathkar ana aamal ana afham*" Given the time, you could teach your men to say it so that it would be recognisable to most Arabs. Unless you are a better linguist than the average sergeant, what you would not do is teach them to understand it. And that is what training is all about, understanding, the happy marriage of theory and practice and the blossoming of that union.

As with discipline, already described as a form of training, your attitude is going to be positive or negative. Positive if it accepts your responsibility to achieve the best for and from your subordinates, if it appreciates that they all need guidance and encouragement, not forgetting praise, if it realises that training is helping people to learn and creating the conditions in which they can do so, if it knows that men will do more willingly those tasks they can do well, if it accepts that they will slide down the occasional snake as well as climbing the long ladders. Or negative, if it believe's that training is someone else's responsibility, if it thinks that as long as men do as they're told they do not need to know why, if it feels that men resent training and some are untrainable anyway, that men do not want responsibility, that you should not have to tell people more than once, that the only way to stop things going wrong is to keep a tight rein. It always worked that way in the past. There is in the theory of training a Law of Recency. The name is unimportant, what it states is that the more recent the experience, the less likely are skills and knowledge to be forgotten. The Law reminds managers of the need to retain and provide practice. If you honestly believe that it is sufficient to tell people only once you have missed the point about training. And incidentally, about communication, too. This is why the time-honoured practice of issuing masses of written instructions (under the guise of training), for subordinates to remember months later isn't on either.

You may study the theory of music under the best teachers, you may memorise the most intricate cadenzas. If you are going actually to play the violin, sooner or later you will have to pull the bow across the strings, and it will sound terrible. No one expects a music student to give a public recital the first time he handles an instrument. No one should expect a constable to give an applause-winning shift the first time he ventures on to the streets, yet it often appears the public do, they do not distinguish between the man with the long service medal and the recruit, notebook buttoned over palpitating heart.

As a manager, you must distinguish, if men are going to develop their talent, they are going to make mistakes. "What! The police never make mistakes". The police may never publicly acknowledge them, it's not quite the same thing. That world famous violinist made a horrible row at the beginning, even if he prefers to forget it. The only pictures by Great Artists we look at are the masterpieces, we never peer into the rubbish bin at the spoilt canvases. Their teacher did, to explain what was wrong. This is not a plea to ignore mistakes, quite the reverse the only acceptable standard is the best. It is a plea not to condemn the first tentative steps, not to laugh at mistakes you may have forgotten you made. A paradox of police training is that most of it can only be done through doing the job among the public where the standard expected is that of the trained man — on the job — training with a vengeance. And as no one can forsee all that might befall policemen, in one sense each incident is different, that training must be left in some respects to the individual himself. With understanding and control he can be allowed to experiment, to learn of the world as it is, instead of how he has been told it will be.

Ideally, training should be a natural progression, a stage not attempted until the previous one has been mastered. You know that in practice this is impossible; there's more than one trembling young bobby run into a bloody affray in his first hour on the beat; some nights nothing happens, the next all hell's let loose; you can go for weeks and never have a fatal accident, you can have three in the same tour of duty.

Experience can be directed through a conscious effort on the manager's part. People will not fall from twenty storey office blocks to order, the man to deal with it when it happens can be selected. It is always tempting to send the fellow you know can handle it with ease, for one thing, it is less trouble to you. Sometimes you can send the man who needs the experience, alone or with someone else, yet perhaps, without reducing the whole section to disarray. Sooner or later, something is going to happen when the only man you can send is the fellow twittering with self-doubt because although it is an everyday occurrence which everyone assumes he can cope with, no-one has actually shown him what to do. He may have been told, but we have already agreed that telling is not training. So if the poor fellow does not do the job to your satisfaction, do not blame him. The fault is yours, together with the trouble of cleaning up his mess. Experience does give confidence and expertise, if it is the right sort of experience. Too many mistakes, too many misdirected efforts, too many unsatisfactory outcomes and feelings of inadequacy are also experiences, which destroy confidence, dilute initiative and injure pride. And this is true for ten year constables and sergeants.

Of course, one argument against training, against giving men experience is that once they're trained you lose them. It is right the subordinates should be pushed on at the first opportunity. Yes, you will have personally invested a great deal of time and trouble in bringing them up to scratch, but that is what you are paid for and the organisation needs its good men in the right places. There may however, be a bonus for you. The high flyers in any organisation look round for the fast road to the top. If that happens to be your section, that is where they will make for, hence the quality of your subordinates should improve.

In deciding who should accompany young constables, either to a single incident or for a whole shift, give a thought beyond who can be spared. "I've told him all I know and he still knows nothing" is funny only on the television, in practice it is disastrous, not for the lack of information but for the attitude it communicates about you, the manager. Are you really that disinterested? Nor are the best practitioners necessarily the best trainers. Initially, young men model themselves on their trainer. It is not only which lights are left burning all night or which is the best place for a quick cup of tea, it is also the communication of attitudes about a hundred and one things connected with the job. Some of your best men may have a shortsighted point of view, be disgruntled, lack patience. You know that your young men are going to pick up enough bad habits of their own without your help. There is someone on your section who can answer the naive questions calmly; who can explain accurately the most important part of the organisation, your section; who can take pride in passing on his craft; who in the words of the poet can be guide, philosopher and friend! That someone may come from an unexpected source, several hard-bitten old sweats have taken on a new lease of life training the next generation of hard-bitten old sweats. The best trainer of all is you. You cannot devote all your time to it, you cannot attend every incident. In the first formative months you should try to accompany men in training as often as possible. Not only will they see you in action, you will see them. You cannot judge a man's attitudes too accurately from a short typed report.

When sending men out in company, make it clear to the learner why he is accompanied, make it clear to the tutor what is expected of him; it is so the learner may get the feel of the vehicle while someone is there to stop him being a danger to himself and others, to teach him to read the road. Establish at the end of the tuition period what has been learnt and what has been taught, not only in the sense that the barrel of beer falling off the lorry was an offence against Regulation 76 of the Construction and Use Regs., but what was learnt from the approach, what was learnt from the drivers' reaction, what the inevitable bystanders thought; whether the policeman would act differently in future.

By now you'll have worked out the proverb: "I hear I forget. I see, I remember. I do, I understand". The doing may need interpretation to become effective understanding, people often need help to learn. This talking about incidents is an effective training medium for all constables, yes, and sergeants too. Provided it is done with some purpose. It is informal, when theory and practice can be drawn together. To the inexperienced they often appear strange bedfellows. If you do not explain, it may be thought that theory is irrelevant or practice wrong. If you promote either of those ideas, others will accept them. You can also share your experiences, you will have met circumstances which are outside their ken and they will be interested in hearing about them, as long as you share the failures and the successes.

This does you no harm, they know you have dropped the odd clanger, if you do not tell them, someone else will, with more than a bit of garnish. You may as well face up to it, unless they have actually *seen* you walk on water they will assume you are human like themselves. Out of all this informal chat someone may ask a question which doubts procedure carried on for no other reason than it has always been done that way. You may also pick out that what is being taught in formal training classes is ambiguous or misunderstood and tell the Training Department. If they are as good managers as you, they will be grateful.

"Hold on! There isn't time for all that on my section, we're too busy doing the job". Not all the time. And if you can reduce the time each job takes, because your section is better-trained, more efficient, happier, less worry to you, is not that worth a few minutes extra now?

No one can be made to learn, before anyone will accept training he must be interested in the job, in improving his professional competence. He may go through the motions to please you or scrape through an examination but his object is not training. With young constables the willingness to learn is usually present for two reasons, the are only too aware of their own limitations which undermines their self-confidence, and part of the price of acceptance by the group is a certain standard of job performance. As the manager, that standard is one you fix. For many young constables their theoretical knowledge of law and procedure is never higher than when they emerge from Training Centres into the cruel world. Slowly it slips away, partly because they do not have the opportunity of practising all they've been preached, and partly because of the malign influence of a certain " University". The fact remains, that it is easier to maintain than regain a standard. Knowledge is power to a policeman, it is the basis from which confidence and job satisfaction grow. Everyone works better if he knows what he is doing, if he feels that whatever is lying in wait round the next corner he can deal with it. As manager, you should encourage your men to keep up this standard. There will be excuses: the lawn has to be mowed, the wife wants to visit her mother, the girl friend demands attention. Despite these pressing problems, you are asking for no more than a couple of hours a week, and not always of study. Critical thought can be just as rewarding. You know that it is hard work which earns promotion or a transfer to the plush seats of divisional administration. Ambition alone is not enough. It is so obvious that it is often overlooked.

If you are interested in training, in improving job performance, so will your section. If you regard training as a barely tolerable intrusion into operational duties, so will your section. If you are willing to answer questions, take time to explain, to discuss, to evaluate, so will your section. If you pay lip service, fob people off, accept second best, so will your section. And what's more, they'll think you do not know the answers.

"Humph! You should see my lot, fifteen years service, cannot pass their exams, practical men bobbying on with no prospects. Interest them in training?" If you are making statements like that, are you sure they've written themselves off or are you doing it for them? Unless you are one hundred per cent satisfied with the way they do their job and that they are working to the limits of their potential, they need training. It may help to make the not untrue assumption that all men have a core of professional interest beneath the veneer of disdain and apathy. Of course, you will have to be subtle, you will have to make allowances for their experience, their dignity, their position as elder statesmen. It will have to be a discreet affair. You may find that your interest and concern are reciprocated. You may find that in part their apathy is rooted in a past lack of training under someone who was not half the manager you are. And it can be emphasised again, this is not a yearly appeal "to take the exam." If he knows he will not pass and you know, he is not going to prove it publicly. You manage your section, you could give these men the chance, under supervision, to be acting sergeant occasionally. It will stretch their imagination, tax their grey matter, and the result may surprise you. They may also gain some appreciation of your problems. Or you could make these men responsible for training younger constables, not just for a night or week, for the whole of their probation. Or you could give them some specific responsibility, say checking certain records are always up-to-date. Whatever it is, it must be useful to the section and obviously so. If you are assessing your men as the good manager you are, you will have some clues on what makes them tick. These may well be the clues to their training problems. Of course, you will have already decided that we are also talking about delegation and job satisfaction. Training is not just preparation for the next rank, important though that is. Not everyone has the ability to be a Chief Constable, not everyone wants to be. Training is wide enough to prepare the promotable and enrich the work of those who in the eyes of the great are destined to remain lesser mortals. There is honour, dignity and self-fulfilment in doing a job well, whatever its rank may be. The ambitious should remember that a man with rank higher than his talent is just as frustrated as a man with talent higher than his rank.

Training is an individual process, people learn at different rates, have different weaknesses, different strengths. Some need showing but once, others need it hammering in a hundred times before it makes much sense. Do not blame the slow learner if he is trying, compliment him on the progress he is making even if you have to look close to see it. The dullard knows his own limitations, if you rub them in too much he will stop trying. Be patient if he is making an effort, he is no more responsible for being a little dim than you are for your brilliance.

Similarly, if you have a "flyer" feed him enough to get him off the ground. Training should be fitted to the man, not the man to the system. With classes of twenty and a somewhat inflexible programme, Training Centres can't give much individual tuition. You can, you have the close personal contact. You can tell a man precisely how you think his training is coming along, you can identify his training needs and arrange for their solution yourself or through the specialists. He can tell you how he thinks he is doing, what he feels his training needs are. You can recommend him for courses, for attachments and additional experience. Your training responsibility is flexible. You have the time. You may even have thirty years to regret the mistakes of your training.

Most men are better at some jobs than others, usually the ones they like doing. The universal genius is rare. What men like doing they will do in preference to anything else, even though the action may not have much call for an expert on swarming bees. Knowing what a man likes doing, knowing what he can do well may indicate his problems in other directions. He is not being lazy, he may not know himself why he prefers accidents to domestic disputes. You may know, you may have come across the same problem before. Once you know what the problem is you are half way to finding a solution. Sometimes the difficulty is no more than a lack of self-confidence. True, he puts on the stern knowing face, underneath he is far from the calm majesty of the law. He will conceal his feelings, more so if he thinks he is expected to be calm and majestic, and he himself may not realise their true cause. You will, if you are a skilful manager. What has just been said applies to all constables, not just the young, the sergeant controlling the section as he thinks you want it done, and you, when you get one of these shall I/shan't I, half welfare/half discipline problems that policemen seem to create to tease you. Lack of knowledge, lack of experience equals lack of confidence. So if he know there's going to be a little job he is not sure what to do with, the safest thing is to leave it alone. What men like doing is what they can do well, the things in which they can achieve some degree of success.

The Americans have a sytem of role-call training. When you take the parade spend five minutes asking questions about the law, about the job. The object is to awaken interest and improve knowledge, not to cause embarrassment, so it may help to give notice of your intentions, a subject of the week. Yes, you are busy and there will be days when you cannot do it. There will also be days when you can. When the novelty and suspicion have worn away, it may make some men open books that have been closed for years, make some think about what they do every day instead of taking it for granted. You may get some suggestions for training or improved job performance, you may have defects in operational and administrative systems highlighted. It will also keep you up to scratch, you will be expected to know the answers to all those questions you're going to ask.

New legislation, new forms, new procedures accompanied by those ponderous memos from Headquarters are ideal for role call training. You know that it was simple for the genius who designed the Found Property Report, Mark MMX. You know that a circle where there should be a cross sends the computer into suicidal frenzy. You know that you can explain to your section better than the mushy instructions full of wheretofores and notwithstandings. The same applies even more to recent legislation, including that which, you are told, is passed to make the law clear. Even if it is a simple Act with less than fifty sections and no words of more than ten letters in the explanatory notes, you ought to make sure your section understand. After all, the lawyers earn fat fees arguing over just one word. It isn't enough to push hundreds out to policemen and expect them to understand perfectly. It is up to you to make sure your section do understand, that you are training.

It has been stated that training is helping people to understand. It is not doing the work for them. Save them needless trouble by all means, don't forget that training requires effort on the part of the pupil. People conditioned to spoon- feeding starve when the spoon is removed. When you are asked what offence so-and-so is, or what section of what Act, tell them to reason it out for themselves or look it up. This is not lack of interest, it is encouraging appreciation, learning, understanding. By fitting incidents they have dealt with inside the impersonal letter of the law, by considering whether certain attitudes are illegal or merely offensive, they are understanding the job. You know that no one can store all the precise knowledge a policeman needs within the average brain, it is important therefore that they learn where to find the information. When they've looked it up, that is the time to talk to them about it, about attitudes, discretion, consequences. If they have done some of the work themselves, something will stick for the future. However, do not let them struggle too long, if your section's twenty year old *Stones Justices Manual* has not the answer, tell them what it is. And in the unlikely event of you not knowing, be honest. They do not expect you to know absolutely everything, you will not fool them if you pretend that you do. They do expect you to find out, you have the authority to ask higher, to keep asking until you get satisfaction.

It is said, mainly by those who have not passed, that the National Promotion Examinations are memory tests irrelevant to the everyday work of sergeants and inspectors. The relationship between theory and practice has already been mentioned — that is not the point. There are able men who should have been promoted, if they had passed. Whatever excuses they now offer, whatever hints of nepotism and golf partners, they have never put themselves into the field from which selections are made. This is a waste of their talent. Promotion study is a hard slog without any guarantee, that's the system. You encourage a man by taking an interest in his studies, not commiserating with his failure. You tell him he will have to work hard, burn a little midnight oil, you offer a little of your time and assistance with difficulties. This is more effective than treating the whole thing as a joke or trying to sell the idea that he does not have too much really and that most of it is luck and all will be well when he passes and it will look good on his record and please the Chief Superintendent and the number of men passing last year was not enough so he had better pull his socks up because the force's reputation is at stake. You know it is not true. Do not insult him by expecting him to swallow it. There is nothing given away in this life to policemen nor anyone else. That includes promotion, and it is not training to pretend otherwise.

Of course, you will have appreciated before this that training is nothing more than good supervision, positive discipline and management to some purpose. Training has been mentioned only in terms of service to the public, the skills and knowledge necessary to provide that service. Once upon a time, as all good stories begin, a section was provided with dictating machines and forbidden to type. It continued to type. Harsh words were spoken, O. & M. men frowned, the typewriters were whisked away. Men who had not held a pen in years laboriously filled foolscap about old ladies locked in lavatories. The number of reports dropped, reflecting the fewer incidents dealt with. It couldn't be the new machines, the inspector reasoned, they were timesavers, the instructions were printed on the side; and he could use them. But he was wrong. Those great hard-bitten coppers who could clear a tap-room in thirty seconds felt flat stupid talking to a machine when there was no one else in the room, they were frightened of what chits of typists would say about them, they did not understand the buttons and coloured lights. Faced with the new paraphernalia they could not think on their feet (which is exactly what a lot of secretaries say about a lot of bosses) so they wrote out what they wanted to say. With impeccable logic, having written it out, there didn't appear to be any reason to have it typed!

The moral of the story is obvious: it is useless to innovate unless people are trained in the use of innovations. Dictating machines, computers, sophisticated communications are in daily use. They are tools, yet not all men take to gadgets. The jibe "gimmickry" often conceals the inability to understand the operation and purpose. Because the Research and Planning Department have worked out a new computer application, it doesn't follow that a generation of policemen educated before the word became current coin will understand. And if they do not understand it, they will not use it. And if they do not use it, it may as well stay in the stores.

Training men in the use of resources in an essential part of every manager's job, the manager should be the first to make sure that they understand any new equipment that comes along. A man does not have to know how a computer works to take advantage of it. He does need training in what is expected from him, and what he can expect from the computer. He does not need to know how a dictaphone works, he does need to know which button to press for what result. You should never take the attitude that some equipment is for "them" and not for "me", therefore you don't need to know about it. There's many a manager succeeded in getting the shop floor swept because he could demonstrate the correct way to use a broom.

If you don't like or do not agree with new methods and equipment, keep it to yourself. After all, it is your job to see that they are made the best of, and it may just be that they turn out better than you expected. If you've sounded off too early, the laugh will be on you. If you've turned your subordinates against them because you were wrong, you've increased your training problems.

That's it on training, there's no apology for not ending with a lived happily ever after, there's no such thing in training; there's always new men, new equipment, new problems to solve, new skills to be acquired, new attitudes to be adopted. Then at risk of being repetitive, no one ever suggested training was easy.

10 Development of the Individual

THE MISSING LINKS

Whatever the type of human organisation, without human resources it won't work; even fully automated plant needs a human finger to press the start button and a human hand to do the maintenance. So on all managers lies the responsibility for use of the human resource, developing it so that the maximum they can contribute is received from each. A manager who fails in this task, fails his subordinates and fails the organisation by wasting resources. Every organisation has people who began their career full of hope, enthusiasm and promise, only to be destroyed by a manager who didn't know, or didn't care, or couldn't be bothered with developing subordinates.

All managers dream that they could be more effective if they had better manpower, better tools, better everything. Successful managers soon learn the simple fact of life, they will rarely have ideal conditions, foolproof equipment or perfect people, they recognise the reality that there must be a trade off between the ideals of what people ought to be and the wide variety of actual talents they bring to the service of the organisation. Training and experience may improve many skills, but by themselves they may still fail to develop people to their highest potential, another job which falls on the broad shoulders of every manager.

The development of individuals has two prongs: one builds up the strengths already there and applies them to the organisation's objectives; the second demolishes the weaknesses to either eliminate them or negative the problems they cause. Everybody's made up of a whole galaxy of vices and virtues, and just as, according to the psychologists, there is no one entirely sane or entirely mad, so in the organisational sense there's no one entirely strong or entirely weak. A manager's first approach is to identify the strengths of his subordinates, then develop them to the advantage of the individual and the job. In any group working on a common task there will be some who shine at some aspects of it, who bring personal qualities to it, like perseverance when everyone else has given up, or a sense of humour which gives the group a lift in times of stress, or an unruffled calm when everything's going haywire. To encourage and develop these strengths not only helps the group performance, it makes people feel their individual contribution is more valuable. Of course, the man who perseveres may be following a cause so lost that all the perseverence in the world isn't going to find it. The man with the sense of humour may need encouraging to use it, may have to learn when it's helpful and when it get's everyone's backs up. The calm unruffled chap may need to sense the times when he should show the iron in his soul. All managers have a wealth of experience, otherwise they wouldn't be where they are in the organisation. Many managers are also misers, they keep their wealth where no one can reach it, believing that finding out the hard way is the only way. Developing strengths may be no more than recognising people's contribution to the job, and saying the right words of appreciation at the right time. It can also be the identification of talent people don't realise they have got, like the natural leader with few chances to lead, and who is so unassuming he does not take them when they're presented. Many people have attributes they consider of no great value, just part of their makeup, what makes them different from the chap next door, attributes which they cannot see how to apply to the job, or fail to realise that they should be applied at all. Often, people fail to see how they can identify their personal aims with those of the job, so their talents are not used very much.

A practical way in which managers can tap under utilised talent and under exploited personality is through assigning workloads consistent with people's growing abilities which allow talent and personality to be used. It is often difficult to achieve when the workload, like operational police duty, is not controlled by the manager, but it is possible with a little give and take and a lot of disappointment and sweat. It doesn't mean loading people down with so much work they have no time to think where they are going or why, and the use of proper management techniques is essential; the correct workload should extend people, stretch their capabilities a little further than they have been before, it should not strain them. Stretched elastic gives good support, strained elastic lets everything down. Things are going to happen over which the manager has no control, his plans will go asunder, some people will not rise to the challenge he's offered. Developing people is a long process, if they've real hidden ability they will not stop learning despite the muffed chances, despite the manager's disappointment and frustration cloaked in continuous encouragement.

Developing people is concerned with job satisfaction, the elusive holy grail of management. The police service begins with an advantage, there is usually some measure of vocation in those who join and stay, and there are within the service diverse avenues through which job satisfaction can be achieved. Never the less, people's job satisfaction reflects to some degree their boss's attitude towards them and the organisation, to find real fulfilment people need a boss who cares about them and the organisation, and who is prepared for the struggle of helping both to contribute to the well being of the other.

Weaknesses in individuals may present a more worrying problem. In some cases, nothing can be done, there are limits to intelligence and ability, there are sides of personality people fight to overcome without much success, attitudes towards certain groups of society, a hasty temper, dislike of routine for instance. Some weaknesses may seem trivial, fear of heights, claustrophobia, but they're real enough to people so cursed who have absolutely no control over their reactions. A positive manager's view of weaknesses accepts the problems exist, and whilst that in itself doesn't cure them, it does prevent mistakes in assigning workloads and tasks. Putting the chap who has difficulty with his temper on the public enquiry desk may well be shortsighted development, if he really cannot control it he will not perform well, and no one will be more aware of it than him.

Some weaknesses can be modified, even eradicated, laziness or lack of attention to detail, even an over hasty temper can be helped by counselling, by encouragement, by praise when the effort's there though the results still leave a lot to be desired. Some times the simple recognition of weaknesses will help, most people have coped with their own personalities for so long they don't present too many apparant problems, and most people can justify the way they are to themselves. The definition of a weakness may be a shock at first, but even though they won't admit it, people will accept the fact if its elimination is in their interests as they see them.

The identification of weakness is not an easy job, especially those that lie deep within the personality, not many people parade them publicly, and if they think it is going to hold back their ambitions, they'll take steps to hide them. It's still crucial an accurate identification is made, for quite apart from not being able to do anything until it's known exactly what's wrong, it's also necessary to separate weaknesses in individuals from weaknesses in the organisational structure. Don't blame delays in the accounting system on the organisation if the people operating it can't add up, and don't blame people if the system is so cumbersome a degree in applied mathematics is necessary and only clerks are recruited.

Weaknesses in the organisation may prevent the development of people more seriously than lack of ability. Tackling these weaknesses presents unique difficulties which no experienced manager needs reminding of, but whenever the opportunity arises, and if it does not he should make it, the manager should make his point known to those who control the working structure. Courage is needed, the experience of industry suggests in fact that managers making these points have little effect, though the small successes in getting a change for the better improve relationships between them and their subordinates who will know that they are not being blamed for something of which they are more victim than offender.

Just as the recognition of strengths involves a trade off between what is desirable and what is available, so too does the recognition of weaknesses. The essence of development is positive realism, seeing people in the round, warts and all, recognising what they are capable of, and what they're not. Positive development builds on the strengths and mitigates the weaknesses, and once the process has begun people can recognise both in themselves in such a way that they want to do something about them. In rare cases, counselling, encouragement coupled with a planned workload and effective training have converted weakness into strength, such miracles do happen. More often, the weaknesses will be reduced so that they can be overridden by the strengths.

Realistic managers do not expect perfection, they hope for it, strive for it, and are used to living with the inevitable disappointments. And they never give up. Any manager, however, despondent about his hard cases, should always to able to think of some good things about them. All managers like to have a moan occasionally, even though it is a waste of precious time, non productive and totally negative. It would be time better spent if they planned how to make more effective use of the strengths available to them. The manager who can see little else to do but moan has a major development problem, a weakness in himself — and that is a good place to start planning a more positive approach.

Conclusion

THE BEGINNING

You have ploughed on to the end, perhaps wondering where it was all leading. You may consider nothing new has been stated, no startling contribution to the behavioural sciences, no penetrating shafts of light on the way policemen do their job, not a single revelation to change the police organisation overnight. Perhaps you feel cheated, here would be the answer to all your problems. You were looking for a blueprint and all you received was a few smudged lines.

You may question what's in management for you. There's been warnings it was not easy, reminders of responsibilities, as if you did not know well enough already. Co-ordinating the skill and talents of other people can be as satisfying as making arrests yourself. Doing a good job through other people can be rewarding, and it is infinitely more difficult than doing it yourself. You will not get many commendations. You will earn respect, perhaps even affection, and that is not to be discounted. You will develop skills as a manager, and they are worth having in any organisation. You will gain new insights and understanding of people, inside and outside the organisational structure, and they're not unimportant. Management is a challenge, as great at the so called lower levels as in the boardrooms of the mighty. Management is not easy, certainly not something you study for six months then sit back for ever. If you are honest, would you really want it to be anything less? Management is people within an organisation, with all the wonder, curiosity and cussedness that human beings are capable of. Individuals, organisations, are born, grow and die. What was true of the organisation yesterday is less true today, and will be even less so in twelve months: new ideas, new equipment, new people bombard the pattern, forcing change, altering attitudes. People conform to no blueprint. If there was a total understanding of human behaviour you could look in the Manual under "Male, 20 years, red hair warts on chin: problem, covets the sergeants' stripes but is bone idle". Happily, that manual is a long way off, until it arrives there will always be a need for managers.

Some of the managerial skills have been dealt with. It is not an exclusive list, you may have come to the conclusion that they are really the same skill, put into chapters for ease of explanation. The cloth of management is woven with many different threads. When you use it, there'll be others waiting to scoff, pointing to your mistakes as proof that management is nonsense, reminding you of the good old days before this new fangled stuff. And they will not just be subordinates. Do not be discouraged, like every manager, in the last resort you are on your own, you will have to weigh success and failure. You will develop your skills to suit your personality, your style of leadership. You will not please everyone all the time, you may please more than the old brigade. You may please yourself a little more often, modestly, and sincerely. You know when that little inner smile is deserved, for in the long run, no one can delude himself for very long.

Every organisation prospers or fails on the skill of its managers, the police service is no exception. Management is an active profession, more than just reading a book. So go out and manage — and GOOD LUCK.

Bibliography

There are many excellent books on management,
among them the following will be helpful:

Easy to read for basic information

Supervision Guides	— Leadership in the factory John Munro Fraser (Pitman)
The Seven Point Plan	— National Institute of Industrial Psychology, Paper No 7
How to Delegate	— G. Holroyde (Mante Publications)
The Techniques of Interviewing	— E. Anstey — Police Journal, April/May 1968

More demanding, but worth the effort

Introduction to personnel management	— John Munro Fraser, (Nelson)
Principles & Practice of supervision	— R.J. Barnes, (Heineman)
The Effective Executive	— Peter Drucker (Heineman)
Staff Appraisal	— Randall, Packard, Shaw & Slater, (Institute of Personnel Management)

For the committed

Explorations in management	— Wilfred Brown (Pelican)
Man Mismanagement	— Alan Fox (Hutchinson)
Principles & Practice of Management	— E.F. Brecht (Longmans)
Organisation World	— Levitt Dill & Eyring (HBJ)
Human Relations at work	— Keith Davis (McGraw Hill)
Practice of Management	— Peter Drucker (Mercury Books)
Personality & Group Relations in Industry	— Michael Fogarty (Longmans)

And one for every manager and managed

Up the Organisation	— Robert Townsend (Coronet Books)

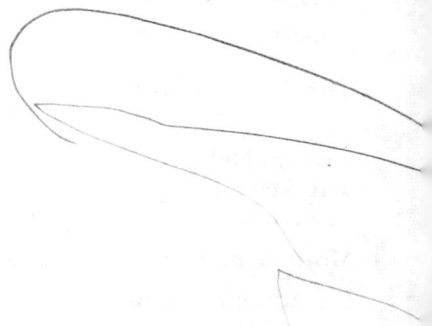